'Sweeping through history and spanning biblical narratives and passages that give us key insight into who God is and our place in God's big story, this is more than a safe companion to Christmas. It is wonderfully moving and inescapably human and had me in tears within the first few pages. Beautifully written, with stories from across the globe and throughout history, *The Whole Christmas Story* holds the reader's hand, pointing us each day towards both the otherworldly and the mundane of human life, with very real and accessible moments that reveal something new to us about the nature of God and our relationship with Jesus. By placing the Christmas story in its wider context, Jo Swinney has done a brilliant job in casting new light on a very familiar story.'
Chine McDonald, writer, broadcaster and head of public engagement at Christian Aid

'Impressive, warming, spiritually fulfilling, this is a warm mug of spiritual nourishment giving plenty to mull on, whether at Christmas or through the year. Swinney's personal tales illuminate nooks and crannies of the Bible, helping us appreciate the first Noel and your current Christmas. Open the book feeling festive and leave feeling inspired. Hugely recommended!'
Paul Kerensa, comedian and writer

'During Advent we can become so mired in shopping and planning, parties and church services, that we lose our focus on why we're dashing round. Jo Swinney's book of Bible-based reflections provides a refreshing antidote as she helps us to step back and take a Google Earth view of God's grand narrative. Build in some time this year to journey with her about why Jesus was born in Bethlehem – your celebration of Christmas will be all the richer and sweeter.'
Amy Boucher Pye, author of Cel

'You've got an Advent treat in store! I was educated, encouraged, challenged and moved. Our journey to Bethlehem begins in Eden, not Nazareth, and ends in a garden city, not Egypt. Jo Swinney reminds us that the Christmas story is part of God's bigger story, and it's one into which we are invited to play our part. It's a whole story for the whole of life. I can't think of a better way to prepare for Christmas.'

Paul Woolley, chief executive, LICC

'With an intriguing sense of adventure, Jo Swinney invites the reader to accompany her on an Advent journey with a difference. With her characteristic curiosity and compassionate eye for hidden details, she leads us to new biblical vantage points on the deep significance of Christmas. Jo's own recent experience of tragic loss also casts a special light on searching questions, like raindrops magnifying the sun's light on a distant horizon. I can't wait for another Advent to read it again!'

Rt Revd Paul Williams, Bishop of Southwell and Nottingham

JO SWINNEY

The
WHOLE
Christmas
Story

AN ADVENT ADVENTURE
THROUGH GENESIS, REVELATION
AND POINTS IN BETWEEN

15 The Chambers, Vineyard
Abingdon OX14 3FE
brf.org.uk

Bible Reading Fellowship is a charity (233280)
and company limited by guarantee (301324),
registered in England and Wales

ISBN 978 0 85746 941 0
First published 2021
10 9 8 7 6 5 4 3 2 1 0
All rights reserved

Acknowledgements
Unless otherwise stated, scripture quotations are taken from The Holy Bible, New
International Version (Anglicised edition) copyright © 1979, 1984, 2011 by Biblica. Used by
permission of Hodder & Stoughton Publishers, an Hachette UK company. All rights reserved.
'NIV' is a registered trademark of Biblica. UK trademark number 1448790.

Scripture quotation marked MSG is taken from *The Message*, copyright © 1993, 1994, 1995,
1996, 2000, 2001, 2002 by Eugene H. Peterson. Used by permission of NavPress. All rights
reserved. Represented by Tyndale House Publishers, Inc.

Scripture quotation marked KJV is taken from The Authorised Version of the Bible (The King
James Bible), the rights in which are vested in the Crown, are reproduced by permission of
the Crown's Patentee, Cambridge University Press.

Every effort has been made to trace and contact copyright owners for material used in
this resource. We apologise for any inadvertent omissions or errors, and would ask those
concerned to contact us so that full acknowledgement can be made in the future.

A catalogue record for this book is available from the British Library

Printed and bound by CPI Group (UK) Ltd, Croydon CR0 4YY

Dedicated to
Thena Ayres and Rebecca Hannan

You hold me up, cheer me on
and inspire me to live a better story.

Contents

4 God among us

5 Redeemed life

Acknowledgements

I want to thank Olivia Warburton at BRF for inviting me to write this book, for her sensitivity and understanding when we had to put the project back a year, and for her encouraging and insightful editing. You have been a joy to work with. I'm also deeply grateful to Carolyn Scriven for her work on my first draft. There are few more gifted and experienced editors in the world and your input lifted my thinking and writing to a higher level. Dan Nolloth, who designed the cover, has a story that mirrors mine in one significant plot twist. His friendship over this season of grief has been profoundly comforting. Thank you, Dan, for blessing this project with your creative ability and me with your compassion and empathy. You are the best.

Acknowledgements

Introduction

WHEN WE TALK ABOUT THE CHRISTMAS STORY, we are generally covering the ground between the angel Gabriel's visit to Mary and the escape to Egypt by Joseph, Mary and the infant Jesus. These events are recounted in the gospels of Matthew and Luke: 120 verses between them. The details are few and familiar. A young virgin suddenly pregnant, her fiancé shamed. A reassuring dream for Joseph and a soothing visit to an older relative for Mary. A journey to a far-off town for a census, the discovery that all guest rooms are full and the newborn Jesus laid in a manger. A visit from some shepherds and the Magi, whose arrival alerts King Herod to a pretender to his throne.

Understandably, at this time of year we think a great deal about this story. You might imagine that a book created to help you engage with the season on a spiritual level would take you through the relevant sections of Matthew and Luke, perhaps coming at them from a new angle or showing them in a different light. There are many wonderful Advent devotionals that do this. I have used some and found them helpful.

But I want to do something different here. I want us to think about how Christmas sits in the whole Christian story, from Genesis to Revelation. I want to take us up a steep and winding path to a high vantage point, from where we can survey the horizon in all directions. Or, to use a specifically 21st-century metaphor, let's play with Google Earth, starting in outer space and zooming in further and further until we are sitting, mesmerised and worshipful, by a makeshift cradle and the God-baby inside it. Who is Jesus, and what is his cosmic significance? Who was he to the generations who came and went before his birth, and who is he to those of us living long after? Why did God take on human form, and what do we do with all those not-completely-fulfilled promises of healing and deliverance?

Please don't expect tidy answers to those huge questions in these pages. They aren't here. But the Bible does take us into the heart of God's purposes for his creation and, if we come humbly and open to the task, he will open our eyes as we read and explore over this Advent season.

On a personal note, I have to confess that, over the years, hearing the Christmas story told in a secular context has sometimes made me cringe a bit inside. It all seemed so far-fetched when given an airing among purportedly rational, educated and sophisticated people: a quaint and primitive fairy story for those willing to suspend disbelief in the name of faith. I wondered if in my heart of hearts, I actually believed it. I suspected it would take a real test to show me my true mettle as a self-professed Jesus follower.

I started work on this book in September 2019. On 28 October, just under two months later, I spent the morning writing. I was on track to hand in a completed manuscript by my January deadline and my mum, who has worked with me on all my books, was in the wings to go through an early draft as soon as I had one to give her.

After lunch, I did a superficial house tidy and packed for a few days away. Around 3.30 pm, I set off with my husband, Shawn, and our daughters, Alexa and Charis, for a half-term break in a remote cottage we had rented. My husband Shawn's phone rang five minutes into our journey, as we were driving down a steep road outside Bath called Brassknocker Hill. It was my uncle Steve, and he asked Shawn to pull over and give him a call back.

Once they had spoken, Shawn got back in the car with red eyes and said we had to go back home. Something really bad had happened, and he'd tell us what it was when we had got into the house. Both girls started crying and asking questions. I told them whatever the news was, God was good, and he loved us and we'd be okay.

The news was life-altering. My parents had been in a terrible car accident in South Africa, where they had been on a work trip with the charity they had founded, A Rocha. My mother had been killed along with two colleagues and friends, Chris and Susanna Naylor. The driver was alive, and my father was in critical condition. I'm so glad I can tell you he miraculously survived with no long-term physical injuries.

Subsequent weeks and months have been painful and dark. Grief hits me like a kind of reverse labour, with contractions coming further apart with time. The intensity of loss can take my breath away, but it recedes and somehow life goes on.

Even at the beginning, when there was barely a second's reprieve from the howling hurt and shock, I had no questions for God. I realised my belief that he was real, he was good and he was loving went deep. I sensed the Holy Spirit brooding over the troubled waters of my distress. Silent, yes, but present, working redemption even as I thrashed around, fearing I'd drown.

My mum loved Christmas. She would start playing wall-to-wall carols on 1 December (we'd banned her from starting earlier), bake dozens of mince pies and spend hours lovingly wrapping the gifts she'd been stockpiling all year. Our Christmas tree was always the best tree of all the trees, and she'd often sit in the glow of its lights late in the evening in childlike delight.

We did our best to celebrate our first Christmas without her, telling ourselves she'd have wanted us to give the grandchildren a happy day. Without her, our clan numbers 17, and we were all together. I'm not sure we celebrated, but we managed to get through it. Christmas without her is never going to be the same.

One thing I know: the Christmas baby has given me a sure and certain hope that one day I will see her again and we will be together in the unveiled presence of the triune God. As Zechariah said after the birth of his own miraculous son, John, Jesus has given us 'salvation through the forgiveness of [our] sins, because of the tender mercy of our God, by which the rising sun will come to us from heaven to shine on those living in darkness and in the shadow of death' (Luke 1:77–79). This is the big picture. This is the context. This is how the whole thing makes sense.

Made whole

A RESCUE EFFORT WAS CARRIED OUT in Chiang Rai Province, Thailand, between 24 June and 10 July 2018 which captured global attention. A staggering 10,000-plus people were involved by the end, including 100 divers, 900 police officers, 2,000 soldiers and representatives from around 100 governmental agencies. Helicopters, ambulances, diving cylinders and pumps to clear more than a billion litres of water from the caves. Many of the rescuers risked their lives, and one, Saman Kunan, died delivering supplies of air. The cost was astronomical, but everyone agreed it was worth it.

What could be worth such costly efforts to save? What deserved rescuing from four kilometres into submerged caves? When I was a child, I had a beloved toy, Norway Doll. At three years old, I would have argued she was worth any effort to retrieve, but the truth is she wasn't. How about an enormously valuable piece of jewellery? Imagine losing the Pink Star Diamond, worth $72 million. You'd want it back for sure, but you'd find it hard to convince anyone to sacrifice their life for it. What about a trapped fox? Or a much-loved dog? They are living beings at least. The harsh reality is that they wouldn't warrant a rescue effort on anything close to the scale I've described either. Trapped in the Tham Luang Nang Non cave were twelve boys and their football coach. Thirteen human lives. That makes sense of all the effort, and amazingly they all made it out alive.

The Christmas story is a pivotal point in the greatest rescue mission ever conceived. As Charles Wesley's carol 'Hark the Herald Angels Sing' puts it:

Mild he lays his glory by
Born that man no more may die
Born to raise the sons of earth
Born to give them second birth.

Jesus was born into danger, hardship and hostility. He lived a life poured out for others and ultimately went willingly to a brutal death, nailed to a cross where he took on the sins of the world. His rescue effort was not understood, sought or even accepted by most, so why did he do it? None of this makes the slightest bit of sense if the object of the rescue wasn't valuable. And so we start our approach to Christmas here, with what is good in creation and with what is precious to God.

1 December

Made good

In the beginning God created the heavens and the earth.
Now the earth was formless and empty, darkness was over
the surface of the deep, and the Spirit of God was hovering
over the waters...

And God said, 'Let the water under the sky be gathered
to one place, and let dry ground appear.' And it was so. God
called the dry ground 'land', and the gathered waters he
called 'seas'. And God saw that it was good.

Then God said, 'Let the land produce vegetation: seed-
bearing plants and trees on the land that bear fruit with
seed in it, according to their various kinds.' And it was
so. The land produced vegetation: plants bearing seed
according to their kinds and trees bearing fruit with seed
in it according to their kinds. And God saw that it was good.

GENESIS 1:1–2, 9–12

How do you remind yourself of important things? I write myself endless notes, send myself texts, get email alerts from my calendar and
rely on people with better memories than mine. And I still find my
mind unable to file things where I can find them when I need them.
At this time of year, things are particularly bad – Christmas parties
where even the host's name is lost to me; finding I can't locate that
thing (what's it called?) that holds up the Christmas tree; failing to put
in the online food order before all the slots are taken; and sending the
kids to school in Christmas jumpers on the wrong day. My grandpa
used to tie knots in his handkerchief as an aide-memoire. I don't know
how he always remembered to put a clean handkerchief in his pocket.

Forgetfulness is not a quirky characteristic of mine – I share it with the rest of the human race. We are by nature forgetful, which is one of the reasons why we have times in the year set aside to remind us of important parts of our story as God's people. Christmas is there for us to remember the birth of Jesus, Easter his death and resurrection, Pentecost the coming of the Holy Spirit and so on. We don't, however, have a built-in way of reminding ourselves, individually and communally, that God made the world and that he made it good. This means we can forget where the story began. And, as you will know if you've ever been late to the theatre and only watched what happened after the interval, if you miss the beginning of the story, you won't fully grasp the significance of its climax and conclusion.

The very beginning of the Christmas story is the beginning of the universe. The Genesis account of creation tells us two things that give crucial context to the part of the plot where God is born a human. First, it tells us God made the world. And second, it tells us the world was made good. Let's consider how these things shed light on the drama in the stable.

Humanist Manifestos I and II state: 'Religious humanists regard the universe as self-existing and not created… we begin with humans not God.' Christians begin with a creator God. It is right there in the opening sentence of the Bible: 'In the beginning, God created.' All physical matter was spoken into being – conceived of, crafted and delivered – by the one being who has no beginning and no end. This is God's show, his stage, his theatre, his everything. Before him: nothing. Without him: nothing. There is a profound connection between creator and created, as artists, parents, builders and inventors all know. If you want to test this premise, see what happens if you tell a chef their food was disgusting. I'd advise you to wear protective clothing for this experiment.

But we are not talking about a plate of coq au vin here; we are talking about the sum total of all matter in the universe. Its maker loves it with a boundless, eternal passion. Why would God stoop to enter the constraints of humanity? Why would he do this with the purpose of submitting to execution? Because he is the maker of this universe, and he was never going to walk away from it.

So God made the world, and when he made it, it was perfect: ordered, harmonious and beautiful. There were boundaries between water and dry ground, night and day. Species were differentiated and behaved according to their design. From formless, empty darkness came a cosmos of infinite complexity, perfectly balanced. He looked at it all and pronounced it good.

Why is it important that we don't omit the part of the story where everything was as it should be? Why does this belong in the same picture as the Christ born into a society where the ruler could issue a command to kill all the baby boys in the area and it would be carried out? Where the few who even claimed to worship God were at odds with each other and more interested in looking good than in what went on in their hearts? Where some were hungry and others over-stuffed? It is important because it sets us off on the right trajectory. The narrative arc is towards redemption and restoration. What was made was so good it was worth saving. Yes, there had been a lot that had gone wrong. Yes, Jesus came because there was a huge mess to clean up. But under the mess, oh what staggering goodness, glory and grace! Jesus was born to carry out a rescue mission because the cosmos was worth rescuing.

For reflection

You are worthy, our Lord and God,
    to receive glory and honour and power,
for you created all things,
    and by your will they were created
    and have their being.
REVELATION 4:11

God willed all things into being. Let your imagination travel around the places you love and know that God shares your delight in them.

Prayer

God of creation, thank you for this beautiful world you made.
Thank you that you are invested in it and that you love it.
You are worthy of all glory, honour and power. Amen

2 December

Meet the maker

The heavens declare the glory of God;
    the skies proclaim the work of his hands.
Day after day they pour forth speech;
    night after night they reveal knowledge.
They have no speech, they use no words;
    no sound is heard from them.
Yet their voice goes out into all the earth,
    their words to the ends of the world.
In the heavens God has pitched a tent for the sun.
    It is like a bridegroom coming out of his chamber,
    like a champion rejoicing to run his course.
It rises at one end of the heavens
    and makes its circuit to the other;
    nothing is deprived of its warmth.

PSALM 19:1–6

Last summer, my girls and I spent an afternoon painting a vase of silk flowers. Alexa, who was twelve at the time, had done an extraordinary job of capturing the colours. Her picture had a serenity to it – unobtrusive brushstrokes, graceful proportions and a harmonious composition. It was careful, pleasing and unchallenging. Charis, nine, had only taken the vase as inspiration in the loosest sense. Her colours were vibrant and unconventional, and the flowers had grown in her imagination. She'd lost interest part way through and the background was left half done, which ended up kind of working. I did mine with a palette knife and it was messy, impressionistic and a bit quirky. We were all painting the same thing, but the results couldn't have been more different, and, without intending it, we'd each revealed a lot about ourselves in our work.

As Christians we talk about having a relationship with God. There are challenges to knowing someone who is not of your kind, is largely silent (or rather doesn't speak using vocal cords) and cannot be seen. But as the apostle Paul wrote, 'Since the creation of the world God's invisible qualities – his eternal power and divine nature – have been clearly seen, being understood from what has been made' (Romans 1:20). One of the ways we can grow in our knowledge and understanding of God, then, is by looking to what he has made.

Psalm 19 says the skies and 'the heavens' (meaning, in this context, what lies beyond the atmosphere, rather than the spiritual realms) reveal knowledge just as clearly as if they were speaking words. The sun gets the full poetic treatment here: it is not merely 'a nearly perfect sphere of hot plasma, with internal convective motion that generates a magnetic field via a dynamo process' (thank you, Wikipedia), but a bridegroom, presumably glowing with the joys of the wedding night, and an athlete at the peak of their prowess, running untiring circuits around the planet – the whole world basking in its rays.

The job of the poet is to spark our imaginations and engage our emotional core, not to spell things out. If we were to try to spell out what the sun tells us about God, what would we say?

God is exciting and dramatic. He could have made a cosmos in which everything faintly glowed, but he made a giant, fearsomely hot and majestically huge combusting ball of flames as our light source.

God is dynamic. He could have made enough suns to keep the place lit up 24/7, but we have one sun that 'rises at one end of the heavens and makes its circuit to the other' (v. 6).

God is breathtakingly creative and cares not just for function but for form. When the sun disappears from view at the end of each day, it didn't have to leave such a feast of colour to feed our souls.

God is a caring, nurturing provider. He made the sun to warm the globe – heat enough for us to thrive but not so much we are scalded.

We who live in a post-Jesus-on-earth era are blessed with the revelation of God in human form; he is 'the image of the invisible God' (Colossians 1:15), the one in whom 'God was pleased to have all his fullness dwell' (Colossians 1:19). The coming of Jesus took the concept of knowing God to a whole new level of intimacy. But it wasn't the beginning of God's revelation of himself and it wasn't the end.

For reflection

Is there a particular place where you feel especially aware of God's presence? What does that place tell you about his character?

Prayer

> Before the mountains were born
>   or you brought forth the whole world,
>   from everlasting to everlasting you are God.
> PSALM 90:2

Thank you for the beauty, the goodness, the generosity and the exuberance of what you have made. You are the creator of all things and all things speak of your character. Open my eyes so I can see more of who you are. Amen

3 December

In God's image

> Then God said, 'Let us make mankind in our image, in
> our likeness, so that they may rule over the fish in the
> sea and the birds in the sky, over the livestock and all the
> wild animals, and over all the creatures that move along
> the ground.'
>> So God created mankind in his own image,
>> in the image of God he created them;
>> male and female he created them.
>
> GENESIS 1:26–27

I love watching medical dramas, especially ones that explore complex ethical scenarios. Is the son obligated to donate a kidney to the dying father who beat him when he was a child? Should you amputate someone's leg to save their life when they have made it clear they would rather die than live without both? Should a loved-up teenage couple who both have cystic fibrosis be kept apart for their own safety? When these no-win decisions relate to fictional patients in a fictional hospital, they are distant enough to be entertaining, not agonising, for me.

The field of medical ethics is becoming ever more fraught as technology develops and enables us to intervene in ways only found in science fiction just a few years ago. At the heart of many dilemmas is this: what does it mean to be human? And how do we evaluate the worth of a human life?

In her heart-wrenching documentary 'A world without Down's syndrome', Sally Phillips visits Iceland, where since 2012 nearly 100% of people have chosen to terminate for Down's. Testing has become easy and accurate, so these babies are identified early. She speaks with a 32-year-old woman named Halldora, who hit the headlines with an article she wrote protesting her right to exist. She is bilingual, has a job and plans to marry her boyfriend. Yet, because of the extra copy of chromosome 21 vast numbers of others like her have been denied their life. 'Who is perfect?' she asked. 'Who can say a person with Down's is worth less?'

For Christians, human worth is bestowed by God. It is the birthright of all Homo sapiens, regardless of capability, skin colour, class or gender. Genesis tells us we are distinct from the rest of creation because we are made 'in the image of God' (1:27). We are not told exactly what this means, although it clearly doesn't mean God has two arms and two legs and all the other body parts we usually have. What we can infer is that something in us all reflects the character of God and can participate in the role of our divine maker in the creation.

However much you love your pet, I'm sure you can see there are some differences between you. My gorgeous kitties can't communicate beyond, 'Food,' 'Where are you?', 'Tickle my tummy' and 'Put me down.' (To you it might seem like they can only say 'miaow', but I have learnt with careful study to understand their language.) They make poor moral choices, like needlessly torturing baby mice, and they are totally lacking in self-control; if there is tuna or cheese on the counter they will jump up to get it regardless of the rules. Humans are different, and that is because God made us like him.

In those first days in Eden, this likeness between humans and God enabled a stunning intimacy of relationship. The man and the woman experienced a closeness with their creator that we can only dream of. The image of God in us was marred when Adam and Eve's disobedience and distrust of God fractured the relationship (an event often referred to as 'the fall'). It only appeared fully once more in the person of Jesus. The process of growing in spiritual maturity is a progressive conformity to the likeness of Christ. And as we become more like Christ, so we become more fully human.

For reflection

How does the person of Jesus help us to understand that we are made in the image of God?

Prayer

Lord, thank you for creating humans so we are able to relate to you, participate in your work and reflect your character to each other. I am sorry for the ways I demean or undervalue the honour of that likeness. Please continue to craft me into someone who looks more and more like Jesus. Amen

4 December

Purpose

God blessed them and said to them, 'Be fruitful and increase in number; fill the earth and subdue it. Rule over the fish in the sea and the birds in the sky and over every living creature that moves on the ground.'

Then God said, 'I give you every seed-bearing plant on the face of the whole earth and every tree that has fruit with seed in it. They will be yours for food. And to all the beasts of the earth and all the birds in the sky and all the creatures that move along the ground – everything that has the breath of life in it – I give every green plant for food.' And it was so.
GENESIS 1:28–30

Walking out of church one Sunday, I was waylaid by a bearer of exciting news. Rachel's son had become a Christian over the summer, the answer to fervent prayers for him throughout his teens. We stopped to chat. Mark had a big decision ahead of him, Rachel told me. He was due to start an engineering course that autumn, but now wanted to do something for God instead. Did I know of any mission organisations that might take someone this last minute? In his mind, engineering was not something you could do for God.

I wonder if you also want to serve God with all your being, time, energy and money, and yet find yourself stretched thin by your 'secular' job, domestic tasks, family commitments and so on. Maybe you comfort yourself with a run-through of your 'spiritual' work: sitting on the board of a Christian charity, volunteering at the food bank or leading a church small group.

The lead-up to Christmas can be straining. We sense this should be a particularly spiritual time of year, but beyond snatching a few minutes to read an Advent reflection (well done – day four and you are still here!), we are more bogged down than ever by life in its unglamorous reality. How, we wonder, can we make sure another Advent doesn't pass us by in a whirl of materialistic distraction? The margins are so tight and, despite such good intentions, life just gets in the way every single year. I feel that frustration and sense of failure too. But I challenge the thoughts that say if I want to give God my focus, I must find a way to strip away worldly concerns, like ordering the turkey and getting a gift for the office secret Santa.

To try to explain why and how I challenge those thoughts, I'd need to start with a question: what does it look like to serve God? Does it mean using accountancy skills to do the bookkeeping for a Christian book-shop? Does it mean leading a church rather than a pharmaceutical company? Does it mean singing in a worship band and not in a West End show?

Genesis 1 tells us the purpose God gave us at the very beginning. He had made a world – a beautiful, precious, complex ecosystem of land, water and air, plants and living things. Among the living things, one species was called out and granted special significance: humans. In verse 28 God gives us a mandate. The mandate is to run the world as his representative: to 'subdue' and to 'rule' on his behalf, as he would do if he was doing it. God brings order from chaos, is committed to the well-being of his creation, is a preserver, provider and sustainer. God offers companionship, brings peace and shows mercy. We serve God by playing our part in running the world in a way that reflects his image in us.

This Advent, our challenge is not to withdraw from the hurly-burly to sit in candlelit contemplation, at least not for weeks on end! Our challenge is to embrace the work of each day as our God-given purpose and to do it as the divine-image-bearer that we are. How does this give meaning to putting the evening meal on the table and washing up the dishes afterwards? What difference might it make to the way I contribute to staff meetings, how I treat the children I teach and the way I reply to emails, stock the shelves, drive the van, change the beds and process the invoices? It all matters. It is all the work of managing God's world on his behalf.

For reflection

How can my work this week be done in a way that reflects its significance in God's eyes? How does the way I carry out my daily tasks reflect God's image in me?

Prayer

Thank you, creator God, for your blessing on us as human beings. Thank you for giving us a part to play in your world, for entrusting us with responsibility for the rest of creation on your behalf. As we approach Christmas, when we remember how you became human, help us to see the worth and value of all you have made. Amen

5 December

Marital bliss

So the man gave names to all the livestock, the birds in the sky and all the wild animals.

But for Adam no suitable helper was found. So the Lord God caused the man to fall into a deep sleep; and while he was sleeping, he took one of the man's ribs and then closed up the place with flesh. Then the Lord God made a woman from the rib he had taken out of the man, and he brought her to the man.

The man said,

'This is now bone of my bones
and flesh of my flesh;
she shall be called "woman",
for she was taken out of man.'

That is why a man leaves his father and mother and is united to his wife, and they become one flesh.

Adam and his wife were both naked, and they felt no shame.

GENESIS 2:20–25

Cherries and baby chub. Colour. Flames. Taste buds, humour and sleep. Caterpillars knowing how and when to make cocoons around themselves, and arctic terns migrating 44,000 miles from one pole to the other every year. The moon. The fact that human skin regrows to heal wounds. These are just a handful of the stupendously amazing ideas that God brought into being. And of all his ideas, one of the best has to be marriage. We are talking marriage as God intended, not marriage as seen on *EastEnders* or *The Jerry Springer Show*, obviously. We will get to thinking about brokenness in a few days, but we are starting at the beginning – when God created everything, and everything was good.

I've always found it interesting that God saw Adam was alone (Genesis 2:18), even though he was in God's presence. How many iterations of the sentiment that all we need is God are there in contemporary worship songs? Approximately a gazillion. But it isn't an idea we find in the Bible. God himself knew we needed our own kind to keep us company. The creation of Eve for Adam was the gift of companionship to stave off loneliness. As Ecclesiastes 4:9 says, 'Two are better than one.' There is a reason prisoners are put into solitary confinement if they misbehave – it is worse punishment than being locked up with other people. Enforced isolation over a long period of time is a form of torture. This is not to say single people can't be fulfilled and happy or that deep relational belonging can only be found in marriage. They can and it can't. However, a good marriage is one of the best protections against loneliness there is.

Eve is also given to Adam as a helper. The Hebrew word here is *ezer* (pronounced *ay-zer*). While the strongest connotations of 'helper' for us are of a supporter or provider of backup, in the Old Testament, *ezer* most often refers to God acting to rescue people. In marriage, God intended us to have a powerful source of strength and support in the other person. Even in the garden of Eden before the fall, there was challenging work to be done. In his invention of marriage, God made this workload less daunting.

Adam needed one of his own kind, and God went one better – the same but different: 'male and female he created them' (Genesis 1:27). Two whole and different people becoming 'one flesh'. They were not replicas of each other; there were genuine differences (any two-year-old will point out some of the obvious ones if you give them a chance). But they fitted together easily and joyfully.

Marriage as God designed it has a secure permanence to it. When the man and the woman are 'united' (v. 24), they no longer belong to their family of origin – their parents – but to each other. A new family unit is formed, and families, as philosophers, sociologists and historians down the ages have agreed, are the foundational building blocks of society. The American diplomat Michael Novak called them the first, best and original Department of Health, Education and Welfare.

God designed marriage to provide companionship, help, intimacy and support for his human creations. In its unity and diversity, love and cooperation, and ability to produce children, a marriage relationship reflects some characteristics of the relationship between the members of the Trinity and foreshadows a time when humankind will be fully united with the triune God. It is indeed one of God's very best inventions.

For reflection

How have the best examples of marriage I've come across taught me about God, about love and about what humans need to flourish?

Prayer

Father God, thank you for your invention of marriage. Thank you that you designed humans to live together in love, commitment and mutual support. I pray for the marriages I know that fall far short of your intentions. I pray for your healing, restoration and peace in hurting families. I pray for those who are lonely to find belonging. Amen

6 December

The harmonious whole

He makes springs pour water into the ravines;
   it flows between the mountains.
They give water to all the beasts of the field;
   the wild donkeys quench their thirst.
The birds of the sky nest by the waters;
   they sing among the branches.
He waters the mountains from his upper chambers;
   the land is satisfied by the fruit of his work.
He makes grass grow for the cattle,
   and plants for people to cultivate –
   bringing forth food from the earth:
wine that gladdens human hearts,
   oil to make their faces shine,
   and bread that sustains their hearts.
The trees of the Lord are well watered,
   the cedars of Lebanon that he planted.
There the birds make their nests;
   the stork has its home in the junipers.
The high mountains belong to the wild goats;
   the crags are a refuge for the hyrax.

PSALM 104:10–18

My husband Shawn and I were driving from Minneapolis back home to Vancouver. Much of the 30-hour journey had been spent crossing the great, featureless Canadian prairies as fast as we could. On our third day we hit the Rockies, and around lunchtime we pulled into a layby to stretch our legs and eat. We were in the folds of the mountain range, surrounded by walls of rock, down which played streams and waterfalls. The grass on the verge was lush underfoot. I took off my shoes and laid down on my back to take in the distant peaks and the blue of the sky. A vast bird of prey passed over my head. Before we got back on the road, we read Psalm 104. We could see before our eyes the goodness and harmony described – God's bounty on full display.

There are times and places like that pitstop outside Banff when, as the old expression says, 'God's in his heaven, all's right with the world.' Those moments give us a glimpse into Eden – the world as God made it to be. Psalm 104 takes us through some of the ways things were designed to work and still work even today when not wrecked by human sin.

Water. Children are taught about the water cycle at school, and it is one of those things we mostly take for granted. But think about it for even just a moment and it will blow your mind. There are inbuilt ways for water to be redistributed and purified. It moves from underground to over ground to sky in a continuous cycle, sustaining life on our planet. In the poetry of Psalm 104, God 'waters the mountains from his upper chambers; the land is satisfied by the fruit of his work' (v. 13). People, animals and plants have their thirst quenched and are nurtured by springs, rivers, lakes, oceans and rainfall.

Food. I have a friend who cares so little about food that most of the time she substitutes meals for powdered nutrient drinks. I cannot begin to understand this. I've been planning what to have for lunch since breakfast, and it is going to be a highlight of my day. God, in his great generosity, made food a pleasure as well as a necessity. He gave us wine to gladden us, oil to make our faces shine (brilliant should oily faces come back into fashion) and bread to sustain our hearts. That speaks of a kind of sustenance far more than is required to keep us upright: joy, comfort, celebration and glowing health.

Home. Psalm 104 picks out three wonderfully diverse species to demonstrate God's provision of a home tailored to suit each one – the stork has the juniper, the wild goats the high mountains and the hyrax the crags. Shrimp don't feature in Psalm 104, but if you've watched the BBC's *Blue Planet II*, you may like me have been entranced by the story of a teeny pair washed into a Venus flower basket, where they grew too big to leave and thus were protected from predators. God made a perfect little love nest for them!

For the first humans, home was a garden full of everything they needed to thrive. God created a place for all of us, a world where the vast array of creatures and plants he'd brought into being could co-exist in interdependence and harmony.

For reflection

As we come to the end of these days spent considering the goodness of all God made and turn towards the damage we've wrought, let's pull off the road and pause for a short while. Let's look around us and pay attention to the incredible design that means any of this is here at all. Let's thank our maker for giving us water, the source of life; for giving us food that keeps us alive and gives us pleasure; and for giving us, and all the other creatures he made, a home.

Prayer

> *May the glory of the Lord endure forever;*
>   *may the Lord rejoice in his works…*
> *I will sing to the Lord all my life;*
>   *I will sing praise to my God as long as I live.*
> *May my meditation be pleasing to him,*
>   *as I rejoice in the Lord…*
> *Praise the Lord, my soul.*
> *Praise the Lord.*
> PSALM 104:31–35

Broken

Aᴛᴄᴇʀ ᴛʜᴇ ɪɴᴄɪᴅᴇɴᴛ ᴡɪᴛʜ ᴛʜᴇ ꜰʀᴜɪᴛ ᴛʀᴇᴇ, things escalated fast. There was murder, rape, theft, war – systematic, ugly behaviour. Theologians often talk about the biblical drama in four acts: creation, fall, redemption and restoration. We're going to sit for a while in the darkness of the fall's fallout. It isn't the most comfortable part of the story. I for one would love to speed through the tunnel and into the bright open space on the far side. But Advent is a season for reflection and preparation. It is a time of waiting and longing and expecting. We are looking with our Old Testament forebears towards the birth of a Saviour, born because the most drastic of measures were needed to mend the brokenness.

I often stumble into Christmas quite unprepared. The autumn passes by at a clip and then suddenly 25 December is a matter of weeks away, and those weeks are filled with issuing and accepting invitations, menu planning, food and gift shopping, and disastrous festive craft projects. Yet again I'm there celebrating the birth of God as a human without a moment's reflection. If I do give it thought, it is often a cheery, here-comes-the-due-date type thought.

We may not relish the thought of paying attention to the darkness, but it is there all around us – part of the picture. Looking at the dark parts is going to sensitise our eyes to the light. When it comes, it will dazzle and amaze us – blazing in glorious, cleansing technicolour.

7 December

Alienated from God

'But our ancestors refused to obey him. Instead, they rejected him and in their hearts turned back to Egypt. They told Aaron, "Make us gods who will go before us. As for this fellow Moses who led us out of Egypt – we don't know what has happened to him!" That was the time they made an idol in the form of a calf. They brought sacrifices to it and revelled in what their own hands had made. But God turned away from them and gave them over to the worship of the sun, moon and stars. This agrees with what is written in the book of the prophets:

"'Did you bring me sacrifices and offerings
    for forty years in the wilderness, people of Israel?
You have taken up the tabernacle of Molek
    and the star of your god Rephan,
    the idols you made to worship.
Therefore I will send you into exile" beyond Babylon.'

ACTS 7:39–43

Adam and Eve blew it. They did the one thing God had prohibited them from doing, and they did it for the worst possible reason – to overreach their already exalted position and become like gods. The first humans enjoyed total trust and total, untainted love in their relationship with God. They experienced God with the closeness of a newborn to its mother in the first moments after birth.

Their act of disobedience and deceit was shattering. In God's mercy, it didn't lead to permanent estrangement, but nothing was ever the same. Like a terrible family feud, the rupture in the relationship with

God passed down generation to generation, each child born inclined towards conflict with their heavenly Father.

Today's passage is part of a speech made to the Jewish ruling council by a man named Stephen, around three years after Jesus had returned to heaven. Stephen was one of the first Christians and he'd been arrested by the religious authorities. Standing before his accusers, he explained what went wrong between God and his people in order to place Jesus in context. Stephen's narrative captures three aspects of alienation from God that continue to play out today.

The first aspect is disobedience. Why is obedience to God so important? And conversely, why is disobedience so damaging? It is hard for us to peel away associations with human authorities when we think about God's authority. I had an ongoing conflict about socks with my dad when I was a small child. I could feel the seams on the ends of my toes and they bothered me. I wanted to wear my socks inside out and my dad wouldn't let me. I still don't understand why! There might have been a good reason, but equally maybe there wasn't. My dad is wonderful, but also human. We may not always understand or agree with God's commandments, but God is not human – he is divine. Obedience is the result of understanding that difference, showing due respect and trusting that God's ways are beyond and above ours.

The second aspect is the active worship of other gods: a golden calf; sun, moon and stars; Molek and Rephan. The Bible speaks of God's jealousy towards his people. True love demands fidelity – it doesn't smile at adulterous behaviour; it howls in pain and rage. We were created to be worshippers, and the only right object of our worship is God. But since the fall we have all been prone to idolatry. In my bit of the world, we may not worship statues, but we give undue time, attention, sacrifice and trust to houses, jobs, sex, food and entertainment, families, savings and investments, beauty enhancement, holidays and lifestyle-enhancing tech: all the things we want for Christmas! Jesus said, 'No one can serve two masters. Either you will hate the one and love the other, or you will be devoted to the one and despise the other.

You cannot serve both God and Money' (Matthew 6:24). Many in our culture slavishly serve money. How about us?

The third aspect of our alienation from God is his granting of freedom to walk away from him: 'But God turned away from them and gave them over to the worship of the sun, moon and stars' (Acts 7:42). God is not a doormat. His mode of relating to humankind has been in the form of 'covenant' – a solemn mutual agreement with commitments from both parties. God has always kept his side of the covenant. But for the covenant to stand, both sides must do their bit.

Stephen's message didn't go down well. In fact, he was stoned for it and is considered the first Christian martyr, his death commemorated by the western church on 26 December. Acts records him crying out in his last moments, 'Lord Jesus, receive my spirit' (7:59). Alienation from God is not inevitable; it is not permanent: the most amazing reunion awaits those of us who long for it.

For reflection

'Once you were alienated from God and were enemies in your minds because of your evil behaviour' (Colossians 1:21). Have you ever felt alienated from God? What was it like? How does it compare to being at peace with him?

Prayer

Father God, all of us have sinned against you: turned away from your love, distrusted your care, disrespected your authority and made other things our priority. Thank you for your boundless mercy and grace that keep the way open for reconciliation. You are worthy of my undivided worship and loyalty. Amen

8 December

Displaced from home

So the Lord God banished him from the Garden of Eden to work the ground from which he had been taken. After he drove the man out, he placed on the east side of the Garden of Eden cherubim and a flaming sword flashing back and forth to guard the way to the tree of life.
GENESIS 3:23–24

In 1943 a philosopher and activist named Simone Weil was given the monumental task of creating a plan to restore Europe after the devastation of war. Everything from sewage to education, from farming to health care needed fixing. Weil began by delineating the qualities of a society in which individuals can survive and flourish. She identified freedom of opinion, order and justice, the right to own property and a common understanding of truth. But she said, 'To be rooted is perhaps the most important and least recognised need of the human soul.'

My hunch is that chronic homesickness is an almost universal condition. We are restless and nostalgic for other places and other times. We wrestle with a sense that we don't belong, with the fragility of impermanence, with heartache for homes we have never had. Stephen King writes, 'Homesickness is not always a vague, nostalgic, almost beautiful emotion, although that is somehow the way we always seem to picture it in our mind. It can be a terribly keen blade, not just a sickness in metaphor but in fact as well.'

Christmas advertising takes our longing for home and leverages it to increase sales of chocolate-selection boxes, gravy granules and train tickets, because savvy marketers know how to exploit our pain. But food, travel, scented candles and carols aren't the fix, because our sickness runs deep. At this time of year, it can be particularly acute, partly thanks to the lingering Victorian fantasy version of Christmas, which has us gathered in jolly family groups around blazing fires in enormous yet cosy drawing rooms.

The Christian metanarrative locates the source of our homesickness all the way back to the garden of Eden. Our distant ancestors knew home. It was a beautiful garden where they lived with God and each other in total peace. The garden was safe and secure, and it provided for all their needs. And in this garden, they both worked and rested, knowing their purpose and role but not overwhelmed by it because God was over and above it all.

And then the fall occurred, and Adam and Eve were banished from their home. They were displaced, exiled, barred from re-entry and left to live out the rest of their days on foreign soil.

Echoes of this story reverberate down the ages. In the time of Noah, the depths of evil were such that God flooded the world and made it uninhabitable, only a floating remnant surviving. Later, at Shinar, humanity gathered and began building a God-defying tower. God scattered them and confused their language. God promised Abraham that he would be the father of a nation and that nation would have a land. Three generations later the growing family was exiled to Egypt to escape famine. They were foreigners and slaves for 400 years, then nomads in the desert for 40 more. When they entered the promised land, it was not to be their forever home. Idolatry and rejection of God led to banishment to Babylon. The experience of exile is in our DNA, our collective memory – buried very deep, but there nonetheless.

In becoming human, Jesus experienced losing a home over and over again: he left heaven for earth; he was born in a town not his family's; he was a refugee in Egypt as a toddler; he lived as an itinerant for his final three years. He understands the pain of homesickness and he was born to heal it. 'Live in me,' he said. 'Make your home in me just as I do in you' (John 15:4, MSG).

For reflection

When did you last feel homesick, and where or what was it for? How do you think the loss of home for Adam and Eve might still be making itself felt in the human experience today?

Prayer

Thank you, Lord God, that although the gates to Eden were barred to Adam and Eve, you found a way to bring us back home. I choose today to make my home in you. Amen

9 December

Wounded and wounding

Furthermore, just as they did not think it worth while to retain the knowledge of God, so God gave them over to a depraved mind, so that they do what ought not to be done. They have become filled with every kind of wickedness, evil, greed and depravity. They are full of envy, murder, strife, deceit and malice. They are gossips, slanderers, God-haters, insolent, arrogant and boastful; they invent ways of doing evil; they disobey their parents; they have no understanding, no fidelity, no love, no mercy. Although they know God's righteous decree that those who do such things deserve death, they not only continue to do these very things but also approve of those who practise them.

ROMANS 1:28–32

Shortly after the end of World War II, an American army officer discovered a photograph album in the abandoned flat he'd moved into in Frankfurt. When he returned home, he took the album with him, and it sat in his basement gathering dust. In 2006, he wrote to the United States Holocaust Memorial Museum, which has since made this extraordinary historical record public.

The album contains 116 black-and-white images of German officers enjoying themselves in and around Auschwitz, Poland. They are pictured sunbathing, cavorting with bright-eyed, shiny-haired young women, feasting and dancing. There are pictures of a picnic, a game-hunting expedition and a candlelit dinner.

Among those identified in these pictures of carefree pleasure-seeking are Richard Baer, commandant of Auschwitz from May 1944 to January 1945; Josef Mengele, the camp doctor known as the Angel of Death, who carried out horrific experiments on prisoners; and Rudolf Hoess, who oversaw the construction of the camp and was its commandant from 1940 to 1943. If anyone could be said to have 'no understanding, no fidelity, no love, no mercy', it was these men, spending their working hours committing unspeakable atrocities and clearly enjoying their leisure time to the full.

The rejection of God leaves a vacuum in the soul. Characters unformed by God can warp and ugly traits spring up and thrive. The 'depraved minds' Paul describes don't just come up with awful thoughts. They result in awful actions: inventive ways of doing evil – Auschwitz and what went on there being a prime example.

'More inhumanity has been done by man himself than any other of nature's causes,' wrote political philosopher Samuel von Pufendorf in 1673. He is right that pain and suffering in this life are more often than not caused by our fellow humans. Think about the last time you were badly hurt. Chances are you were damaged by a some*one* not a some*thing*.

But evil does not only exist out there, in the Nazis, sex-traffickers and internet scammers. Look again at this list: wickedness, evil, greed, depravity, envy, murder, strife, deceit, malice, gossip, slander, arrogance, boastfulness and disobedience of parents. Ever wished you had a kitchen like your friend's? Passed on a juicy titbit of unverified information about someone? Participated in a character assassination of your terrible boss? The list makes me burn with shame, because I know a whole lot of those words can be applied to me. And I know that in a normal week, both unintentionally and totally deliberately, I hurt people. I am wounded, and I inflict wounds.

Jesus was born into a world where relationships are risky. He made himself vulnerable to harm at the hands of humanity and experienced rejection, abandonment, mockery and betrayal – not just by enemies but also by his family and closest friends.

Advent is a time of waiting, a time of anticipation and a time of preparation. We are waiting for Christmas, but in a greater sense we are waiting for more: the fulfilment of what that baby's arrival set in motion. Jesus ensured our acceptance and forgiveness by God, but we are still damaged and damaging. He told his followers he would come back once more to finally end all sin and suffering, and so we continue to wait.

The world needed him, and he came. And the world needs him to come again.

For reflection

Bring before God the most painful relationship in your life. Ask him to soothe and heal your open wounds and enable you – in the power of his Spirit – to forgive the perpetrator.

Prayer

Father God, thank you that you can bring restoration into the very worst relationships and that you can redeem the most depraved and evil people. This world is broken and so many of our interactions are painful, but all is not lost. Thank you for coming into the middle of it all to show us a different way. Amen

10 December

Abusing creation

See, the Lord is going to lay waste the earth
    and devastate it;
he will ruin its face
    and scatter its inhabitants –
it will be the same
    for priest as for people,
    for the master as for his servant,
    for the mistress as for her servant,
    for seller as for buyer,
    for borrower as for lender,
    for debtor as for creditor.
The earth will be completely laid waste
    and totally plundered.
        The Lord has spoken this word.

The earth dries up and withers,
    the world languishes and withers,
    the heavens languish with the earth.
The earth is defiled by its people;
    they have disobeyed the laws,
violated the statutes
    and broken the everlasting covenant.
Therefore a curse consumes the earth;
    its people must bear their guilt.
Therefore earth's inhabitants are burned up,
    and very few are left.

ISAIAH 24:1–6

When we think about relationships broken by the fall, we often focus on those between humans and God and between humans with each other. But there is a third relationship that is broken – that of humans with the world.

God's design was for a delicately balanced interdependence between his image-bearers and the rest of creation. When we play our God-ordained role, everything flourishes. One of my favourite childhood books is *The Secret Garden* by Frances Hodgson Burnett. A man makes a beautiful walled garden for his wife. Following her tragic death, he seals the entrance and for years it lies untended. The garden doesn't do well on its own and it takes the intervention of three children to bring it back to its former glory. You might think untouched, virgin woodland would provide a far superior habitat for birds, mammals and insects. However, many studies have shown managed woodlands have greater biodiversity and healthier ecosystems. Likewise, when we mistreat and neglect our environment, everything suffers.

Isaiah 24 starts with judgement from God, highly reminiscent of the earth's destruction by flood in the days of Noah: 'the Lord is going to lay waste the earth and devastate it' (v. 1). But it quickly becomes apparent that this time, all he will do is allow humans their freedom to behave as they will: 'the earth is defiled by its people' (v. 5). The 'laws', 'statues' and 'everlasting covenant' that were and continue to be flagrantly broken were given by God for the good of the whole of creation. The consequences of breaking them are felt by the whole of creation: 'therefore a curse consumes the earth' (v. 6).

Isaiah was writing in the early 8th century BC. I doubt even he could have imagined the damage we've managed to do since then. 'From the pollution-infested landscape of urban areas to the leached soil of decimated rain forests, the human race has exerted its will on the environment with reckless abandon,' says the blurb on *Earth Cancer* by Van B. Weigel (Praeger, 1995). 'In effect, humankind has become a most dangerous type of Earth Cancer. Now this rampant form of cancer is threatening the very existence of life on this planet.'

Van B. Weigel is not the only one to compare humankind to cancer. It isn't an entirely far-fetched metaphor, but it is not a metaphor God would use. There is nothing redeemable about cancer cells. They must be cut out in surgery, poisoned by chemotherapy or obliterated by radiation or they cause death.

We are not cancer cells, but in our sin we can do untold harm. We do not just relate to God and each other, but we also relate to the earth and its non-human inhabitants. These three relationships are inter-connected: when humans abuse the planet, they anger the God who made it, who loves it and to whom it belongs. When humans abuse other humans, this also hurts God and the planet – the environmental devastation of war is catastrophic. We 'bear our guilt' (v. 6) in the consequences of our poor choices and behaviour.

Isaiah has some dark pronouncements, rather out of kilter with the seasonal mood generated by the school plays, drinks parties and omnipresent fairy lights of mid-December. This judgement, this word 'the Lord has spoken' (v. 3), is a bitter pill to swallow, though swallow it we must if we are to be healed.

For reflection

In what ways is your relationship with creation broken? And where do you see signs of hope and restoration?

Prayer

Lord God, maker of the heavens and the earth, sustainer and redeemer of all things, thank you for your creation. I am so sorry for the ways I have damaged your world – through my greed, laziness and arrogance. Please show me how to live here in a way that honours you and fulfils my mandate to steward this planet. Thank you for your mercy, grace and patience. Amen

11 December

Broken bodies

So Satan went out from the presence of the Lord and
afflicted Job with painful sores from the soles of his feet
to the crown of his head. Then Job took a piece of broken
pottery and scraped himself with it as he sat among the
ashes.

His wife said to him, 'Are you still maintaining your
integrity? Curse God and die!'

He replied, 'You are talking like a foolish woman. Shall we
accept good from God, and not trouble?'

In all this, Job did not sin in what he said.

When Job's three friends, Eliphaz the Temanite, Bildad
the Shuhite and Zophar the Naamathite, heard about all
the troubles that had come upon him, they set out from
their homes and met together by agreement to go and
sympathise with him and comfort him. When they saw him
from a distance, they could hardly recognise him; they began
to weep aloud, and they tore their robes and sprinkled dust
on their heads.

JOB 2:7–12

Jonny Kennedy was born with no skin on his right leg. He had the rare
genetic condition dystrophic epidermolysis bullosa, which meant the
very slightest touch caused him to burn and blister. 'My skin is like
Velcro without the hooks,' he explains in the 2004 Channel 4 documentary about his final months. *The Boy Whose Skin Fell Off* has to
be one of the most vivid and intimate records of extreme physical
suffering ever made. If you've seen it, I'm sure that, like me, you've
been unable to forget the scene where his mother Edna changes his

dressings to the sound of her son's howls of anguish. When he died, at the age of 36, there was a palpable sense of relief amid the grief. To watch someone you love in constant, extreme pain is its own form of torture.

Job's friends all wept at the very sight of him. That they tore their clothes, highly valuable in an agrarian society, shows the depth of their emotional response to his suffering. Job too had a horrific skin condition – painful sores from head to toe. In these few verses, we are told both that his suffering was inflicted by Satan (v. 7) and that it came from God (v. 10). It is hard to hold these two thoughts together, but if we take the authority of scripture seriously we have to. The idea that God is somehow implicated in our suffering, whether directly or indirectly in his allowing it to happen, is thoroughly biblical. It is one of those things that fall beyond our ability to understand and, like Job, we can only say, 'I know that you can do all things; no purpose of yours can be thwarted' (Job 42:2).

Pain was one of the curses of the fall – 'I will make your pains in child-bearing very severe; with painful labour you will give birth to children,' says God in Genesis 3:16. I've had two children, and it was indeed severely painful, both times. I also suffer from infrequent but powerful and debilitating migraines. I'm sure you have experienced pain too. We have millions of sensory neurons in our bodies, mostly doing a wonderful job of communicating the information necessary to keep us out of harm's way. But they mean we are vulnerable, and when things go wrong they hurt. To live is to experience pain.

In acute pain, we have a choice. Job's wife articulated the response that is perhaps the most natural: 'Curse God and die' (v. 9). The pain has the final say – it kills faith, hope and love and then it snuffs out life itself. The alternative is acceptance and a gritty determination to cling to God regardless of the agony he has allowed. Job accepts both trouble and good from God and in doing this, we're told he 'did not sin' (v. 10).

We know Christmas is coming because it is a day chosen to mark an event that happened two millennia ago. As we wait for the second coming, the time and date of which we do not know, we need faith, trust and hope. Our broken, hurting bodies cry out for relief. It is hard to witness the physical suffering of others, and it is sometimes tempting to give up and curse God. Let's pray for strength to hold on and wait for the Lord.

For reflection

How have you related to God in times of physical pain?

Prayer

Answer me, Lord, out of the goodness of your love;
in your great mercy turn to me.
Do not hide your face from your servant;
answer me quickly, for I am in trouble…
But as for me, afflicted and in pain –
may your salvation, God, protect me.
I will praise your name in song
and glorify you with thanksgiving…
The poor will see and be glad –
you who seek God, may your hearts live!
Lord, hear the needy
and do not despise your captive people.
Amen

From PSALM 69:16–17, 29–30, 32–33

12 December

Suffering in mind

Lord, do not rebuke me in your anger
  or discipline me in your wrath.
Have mercy on me, Lord, for I am faint;
  heal me, Lord, for my bones are in agony.
My soul is in deep anguish.
  How long, Lord, how long?

Turn, Lord, and deliver me;
  save me because of your unfailing love.
Among the dead no one proclaims your name.
  Who praises you from his grave?

I am worn out from my groaning.

All night long I flood my bed with weeping
  and drench my couch with tears.
My eyes grow weak with sorrow;
  they fail because of all my foes.

Away from me, all you who do evil,
  for the Lord has heard my weeping.
The Lord has heard my cry for mercy;
  the Lord accepts my prayer.
All my enemies will be overwhelmed with shame and
anguish;
  they will turn back and suddenly be put to shame.

PSALM 6

One of my French A-level books was the satirical novel *Candide* by Voltaire. The eponymous protagonist faces misfortune after misfortune with bulletproof optimism and unwavering loyalty to one simple principle: 'All is for the best in this best of all possible worlds.' Being a Christian does not mean turning a blind eye to the facts. We do not need to spin reality to make it look better than it is. Some things are broken and painful, and it is perfectly fine to admit that. Christmas is one of the worst times for people suffering from mental health conditions, and that is partly because of the pressure to put on a jolly face and not spoil the fun for everyone else.

So let's just acknowledge here that part of the post-fall brokenness is human suffering in mind and soul. There is no need to hide that fact under tinsel – it is what it is. The psalmist says, 'My soul is in deep anguish' (v. 3). He gives poetic expression to the darkest of thoughts. If you have experienced depression, anxiety, bipolar disorder, post-traumatic stress or any other illness of the mind, you may resonate with the desperate cries for relief here: 'Have mercy on me… How long, Lord, how long?' Those in the throes of mental health problems more than anyone need healing, delivering and saving.

My first encounter with depression was when I was 13. If you could get credit for time in the pit, by the time I was in my mid-20s I'd have been laughing (through my tears). Now in my early 40s and having got all the help on offer, I am significantly better if long enough in the tooth to know not to take anything for granted.

Depression is very hard to explain to someone who has never been struck down by it. Let me try to mobilise some imagery that might help if you are one of the fortunate few for whom it remains a mystery. Imagine being laid in slowly setting cement. Imagine being untethered from your rocket and left to float in outer space. Imagine you are living inside a dead body. Imagine you have tight metal bands around your head and chest. Imagine you have eaten a big pile of rocks. Imagine you are lost in deep, grey fog. That is how depression and anxiety feel.

The psalmist, writing long before the birth of Christ, nonetheless can say, 'The Lord has heard my weeping. The Lord has heard my cry for mercy; the Lord accepts my prayer' (vv. 8–9). How did God comfort and reassure him?

Centuries after the birth of Christ, here we are with a worldwide epidemic of depression far worse than at any other time in history. What is going on? Didn't Jesus come to fix the brokenness? Why are we still so sad and sore? The answers have to do with the nature of time and the character of God, and they are not simple. But for now, we can say with confidence that God sees and cares about our weeping, groaning and mental anguish. We can be honest with him and each other about our struggles. And we can trust his love, which brought him into the depths to suffer with us.

For reflection

How has your experience of mental health issues (your own or those of someone you know) shaped your relationship with God?

Prayer

God, sometimes the dark is so dense I can't see a single reason to be hopeful. I choose to believe there is no dark you cannot penetrate. Thank you that you have promised you are with me and your word is to be trusted. I'm impatient for healing, for relief, for the morning to come. Help me wait patiently. Amen

13 December

Broken cisterns

'My people have committed two sins:
They have forsaken me,
    the spring of living water,
and have dug their own cisterns,
    broken cisterns that cannot hold water...

'As a thief is disgraced when he is caught,
    so the people of Israel are disgraced –
they, their kings and their officials,
    their priests and their prophets.
They say to wood, "You are my father,"
    and to stone, "You gave me birth."
They have turned their backs to me
    and not their faces;
yet when they are in trouble, they say,
    "Come and save us!"
Where then are the gods you made for yourselves?
    Let them come if they can save you
    when you are in trouble!
For you, Judah, have as many gods
    as you have towns.'

JEREMIAH 2:13, 26–28

We've had a bleak few days, haven't we? Alienation from God, damaged relationships with each other, a battered and depleted planet, the suffering of physical and mental pain – so much has gone wrong. And then there's the kicker – the foolish ways we've tried to fix the situation.

The near Middle East has a long, hot, dry summer, which to those of us non-farming northern hemispherers might sound very nice, especially in the dark days of mid-December. However, this can mean severe water shortages, and you can't live without water.

Jeremiah's first audience would have felt the sting of the illustration in verse 13. A cistern was a way of gathering rainwater to carry you through a dry spell. Cisterns were pits dug into rock – around Jerusalem a soft layer of limestone – and covered in a lime paste to prevent the water seeping out. They frequently developed cracks. Even if they didn't, the water would stagnate and gather debris. Not only were the Israelites choosing to get their water from a cistern instead of a spring, where the water is fresh and clean, but their cisterns were broken.

To put their choice into a more familiar context, say you have been camping for two weeks in the middle of nowhere. You have mud under your fingernails, bugs stuck in your tangled hair and you stink to high heaven. You have the choice between using a shower with unlimited hot water, shampoo and a scrubbing brush or using a pack of baby wipes. You go for the wipes.

Or your car breaks down at the side of the motorway. You can call out a rescue service, who will send an engineer with all the appropriate kit to get you on the road again, or you can get your friend Brian to cycle down the hard shoulder with his bicycle puncture repair kit and some banter. You message Brian. This is how foolish it is to turn to anyone but God for redemption.

God's people, the Israelites, lived with much the same brokenness we do, and their solution was to make some wooden and stone father-figures! When we are in trouble, who and what we turn to for help makes all the difference. What are your leaky cisterns? This passage is not saying we can't take medication and get therapy for depression, or that we shouldn't save to provide for ourselves in old age. What Jeremiah is talking about is on a grander scale. The source of life and health and joy and peace is God himself. The Israelites had prophets with megaphones, but they couldn't and wouldn't hear what those prophets had to say. How about us?

For reflection

Slaking a raging thirst can only be achieved by drinking something. Food, medication or distraction won't do any good at all. In the same way, our spiritual thirst can only be helped by gulping down the water of life – God himself. Sit quietly and ask the Holy Spirit to help you see that your deepest craving is for nothing less than the holy triune God.

Prayer

Thank you, Father, Son and Holy Spirit, for creating us with an inbuilt thirst for your presence. Forgive us for trying to satisfy that thirst in the wrong ways, and help us to come to you, the living water. Amen

Waiting in hope

AFTER LEAVING SCHOOL, I spent just under a year in rural Zimbabwe. The school where I had been posted was a four-hour bus ride from a tarmacked road and six hours from the nearest town of significant size. One weekend, my friends and I went to the bus stop to catch a bus. After a few hours, we asked the man in the bottle store nearby if he had any information on when or whether the bus might arrive. 'It is coming very soon,' he said cheerfully. 'The rains have made the roads muddy, but it is coming!'

Three days later, we were still waiting. Fed by a constant diet of hopeful updates from our friend at the bottle store, we hadn't given up on the idea of a visit to the town for a hot shower and a soft bed. While hope remains, waiting is hard but bearable.

The evils and suffering of the Jewish people as described in the Old Testament are tempered by a growing sense of hope that help is on the way. From Genesis 3:15, where Satan is told his days are numbered and his head will be crushed by a descendent of Adam, to the incredibly specific and detailed messianic prophecies in Isaiah, a picture builds of a Saviour who will restore their relationship with God, bring life and healing, and usher in a new kingdom where righteousness, justice and mercy will prevail. Things were hard, but they waited in hope.

For the next few days, we are going to imaginatively inhabit a world where Jesus is yet to be born. We will be anticipating, scanning the horizon for signs of a coming rescue, looking at the clues about our Saviour's identity.

Christmas might feel a long time away for the children in your life, but what would it feel like to wait when it could be in a few months or it could be three centuries away? How it feels has everything to do with our level of hope. And we can either starve or nurture hope.

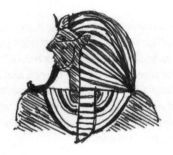

14 December

Reasons to be hopeful

But as for me, I watch in hope for the Lord,
　I wait for God my Saviour;
　my God will hear me.

Do not gloat over me, my enemy!
　Though I have fallen, I will rise.
Though I sit in darkness,
　the Lord will be my light.
Because I have sinned against him,
　I will bear the Lord's wrath,
until he pleads my case
　and upholds my cause.
He will bring me out into the light;
　I will see his righteousness.

MICAH 7:7–9

The job of Old Testament prophet must be one of the most gruelling, thankless, demoralising and poorly compensated in all of history. Prophets had to speak hard words to people actively trying to ignore them; they carried the burden of knowing what would happen if they couldn't get through and inspire repentance; and the authorities considered them at best a pain in the neck, at worst criminally disruptive.

Micah was a prophet in Jerusalem at a time of great prosperity. The city was a bustling hub of commerce and ostentatious religiosity, corrupt from top to bottom: 'Her leaders judge for a bribe, her priests teach for a price, and her prophets tell fortunes for money' (3:11). While the inhabitants of Jerusalem went about their business in smug self-satisfaction, telling themselves God was super happy with them, Micah was close to despair. He was full of both God's love and God's judgement, and the coming disaster almost broke him: 'I will weep and wail; I will go about barefoot and naked. I will howl like a jackal and moan like an owl' (1:8).

What we hear in today's reading, though, is not despair or anything close to it. We hear confidence and trust in the ultimate prevalence of good. Micah has fallen and sits in darkness, but he is able to tell his enemies with bold defiance, 'I will rise… The Lord will be my light' (v. 8).

Micah had phenomenal confidence in God for three reasons.

First, he was well versed in God's track record. He knew what God had done before, which enabled him to predict how he would act in the future. It is impossible to overestimate the significance of the Israelite escape from Egyptian slavery to their identity and relationship to God. The plagues, the passing over of the angel of death, the parting of the Red Sea, the water from the rock and the manna from the sky, the fire and the cloud that led them through the desert – these wonders nourished their faith for generations. And they are our stories too – part of our inheritance as adopted children of Israel. We worship a God who is mighty, powerful, loving and present. He made a way in the wilderness in the past. He can do it again.

When Micah was alive, the Genesis promise that one day evil would be defeated was not yet fulfilled. Did you catch the reference to snakes (v.17)? For us, it is a done deal. Jesus is the ultimate proof that God keeps his promises.

Second, he knew God's character. He knew it because of the stories of old and he knew it because of his own relationship with the Almighty. Look at the divine attributes mentioned in these verses alone: righteous, forgiving, merciful, compassionate, faithful, loving. Do these ring true to your experience of God? What would you add?

Third, he knew God had reliable witnesses who could testify to his character. When we want to know if we can trust someone, we'll often turn to people who know them well for a reference. Are they who they purport to be? Can they be trusted? Micah turns to his ancestors, Jacob and Abraham (v.20).

The days are dark, and we may wonder if we will ever rise from the dirt where we have fallen. In those moments when we are tempted to doubt, let's be spurred on by these words from Romans:

> We also glory in our sufferings, because we know that suffering produces perseverance; perseverance, character; and character, hope.
> ROMANS 5:3–4

For reflection

What are you doing to nurture hope? What reasons do you have for confidence in God's faithfulness to you, those you love and his whole creation?

Prayer

Father God, sometimes you ask us to hold on to your goodness and love in blind faith and in the face of what seems to be evidence of your desertion. Help me to remember your deeds in the past, your character and your many fulfilled promises. I choose to trust you today. Amen

15 December

Hoping for forgiveness

Surely he took up our pain
    and bore our suffering,
yet we considered him punished by God,
    stricken by him, and afflicted.
But he was pierced for our transgressions,
    he was crushed for our iniquities;
the punishment that brought us peace was on him,
    and by his wounds we are healed.
We all, like sheep, have gone astray,
    each of us has turned to our own way;
and the Lord has laid on him
    the iniquity of us all...

Yet it was the Lord's will to crush him and cause him to
suffer,
    and though the Lord makes his life an offering for sin,
he will see his offspring and prolong his days,
    and the will of the Lord will prosper in his hand.
After he has suffered,
    he will see the light of life and be satisfied;
by his knowledge my righteous servant will justify many,
    and he will bear their iniquities.

ISAIAH 53:4–6, 10–11

When I was growing up, our family had a cassette of the music from *Les Misérables*. When one side finished playing, we turned it over to play the other side. Eventually, the tape got chewed up too thoroughly for even the old pen trick to work its magic. By then we knew all the words and had read aloud a child-friendly abridged version of Victor Hugo's original masterpiece. In my early teens, I saw the musical in the West End and I read the proper book, albeit in translation. So where else would I turn for an illustration of the problem of sin and the solution of forgiveness?

First, some things to notice in our reading today. We, humanity, have corporately and individually gone terribly wrong. There has been no discernible progress generation to generation on this front, whatever we'd like to tell ourselves about 21st-century superiority.

The words used for our problematic behaviour here are 'transgressions' and 'iniquities'. Against whom have we transgressed? Towards whom have we been iniquitous? Each other, yes, but primarily towards God. These behaviours are damaging to relationships. Consequences are built into actions: the law of cause and effect.

The protagonist in *Les Misérables* is a man called Jean Valjean, who has two crimes on his slate. For the theft of a loaf of bread, he has served 19 years before finally being released on parole. He breaks parole, changes his identity and is pursued by his former guard, Inspector Javert, for year upon year. In Javert's eyes, he has not paid for his crime in full. Justice remains undone. Javert behaves as though the theft had been from him and of something of far greater value than a baguette. If we are honest, we can behave like Javert when it comes to the wrongdoing of others.

Thankfully, God is more like one of the other characters, the bishop of Digne. Valjean's other crime is stealing silverware from this kindly man who gave him shelter. Caught and brought before the victim of his crime, Valjean expects to be returned to the galleys, but is instead met with forgiveness and the chance to reset his course. 'The silverware was a gift,' the bishop tells the police. 'It belongs to him, so please let him go.'

While there may be parallels, this story of course falls far short of the lengths God went to in order to deal with the problem of our sin. Even if the bishop had gone to prison in Valjean's place, it wouldn't come close. The servant in Isaiah 53 was stricken, afflicted, crushed, wounded, oppressed and finally killed. And this servant had done nothing wrong. 'He had done no violence, nor was any deceit in his mouth' (v. 9).

Old Testament Jews were under no illusion about the issue of their disobedience and failings, and they had been promised forgiveness. The idea of substitution was written into the law of Moses – animal sacrifices were made by penitents. But here in this passage is a hint at a radical and all-encompassing solution: not a lamb but a man. A man who would take punishment on our behalf, clearing our debt to God. They had a reason to hope for real and lasting forgiveness.

For reflection

How do you understand the connection between things you have done wrong and what Jesus experienced on the cross?

Prayer

Lord God, thank you for your breathtaking mercy and kindness. Thank you that there is nothing I have done or left undone that wasn't dealt with by the suffering of the unblemished sacrificial lamb, Jesus Christ. Help me absorb the magnitude of what you have done for me. Amen

16 December

Hoping for justice

Truth is nowhere to be found,
    and whoever shuns evil becomes a prey.

The Lord looked and was displeased
    that there was no justice.
He saw that there was no one,
    he was appalled that there was no one to intervene;
so his own arm achieved salvation for him,
    and his own righteousness sustained him.
He put on righteousness as his breastplate,
    and the helmet of salvation on his head;
he put on the garments of vengeance
    and wrapped himself in zeal as in a cloak.
According to what they have done,
    so will he repay
wrath to his enemies
    and retribution to his foes;
    he will repay the islands their due.
From the west, people will fear the name of the Lord,
    and from the rising of the sun, they will revere his glory.
For he will come like a pent-up flood
    that the breath of the Lord drives along.

ISAIAH 59:15–19

Christmas God goes down far better than Easter God in a secular liberal society. The baby Jesus in his manger can be safely swaddled in notions of love, acceptance and tolerance of pretty much everything.

We coo over him along with the shepherds, wise men and angelic host without disrupting our lives at all.

My society, in 21st-century Britain, has a thousand-year-old democracy. Before becoming one of the worst-hit nations in the world during the Covid-19 pandemic, we experienced decades of prosperity and peace. We've been taken care of by the National Health Service, educated by the state and protected by a benign legal system. Unsurprisingly, we are far more comfortable with the idea of a God of love than a God of love *and* judgement. We don't see the need for anyone to get judgey.

But the Jews were not waiting for a downy-headed baby who would grow up to tell everyone that anything goes and to just calm down. They had experienced terrible suffering at the hands of other nations (and inflicted plenty of their own): 'We all growl like bears; we moan mournfully like doves' (v. 11). How could they respect or love a God who could stand by, uncaring, in the face of atrocity? They were looking for deliverance and waiting for a warrior-redeemer.

Israel was longing for a messiah who would bring justice in the sense of punishment for crime: 'According to what they have done, so will he repay wrath to his enemies and retribution to his foes' (v. 18). If we were Cambodians under Pol Pot, Ugandans under Idi Amin or Russians under Stalin, we'd no doubt be hoping for the same.

Neither the love-only God nor the judgement-only God are real. They are both idols crafted from human need. The one true God, revealed through scripture and creation, made incarnate in Jesus, alive in us through the Holy Spirit, is an endlessly mysterious marriage of justice and mercy. This is a God of vengeance, zeal, wrath and retribution (vv. 17–18). Those who do wrong must rightly fear the consequences. As it says in Hebrews 10:31, 'It is a dreadful thing to fall into the hands of the living God.' And yet, Isaiah's prophecy hints that this judgement will not be enacted in the way the wronged party might hope. The Lord is the one to achieve salvation (v. 16). The armour he puts on is the breastplate of righteousness.

As Israel waited for their redeemer, the prophets painted a picture so detailed and vivid that those with eyes to see were able to recognise him in the carpenter from Nazareth. Of course, there were plenty who rejected him. There are plenty who still reject him. But for those of us who have come to call him Saviour, there is no more stumbling in the darkness and no more need to fear either punishment or no punishment. The 'pent-up flood' of Jesus Christ has washed away the sins of the world.

For reflection

Are you more inclined to focus on the love or the judgement of God? How does the life, death and resurrection of Jesus speak of both aspects of the divine nature?

Prayer

Holy God, you do not overlook the pain, suffering and abuse we inflict on each other. Our sin offends and angers you, because you are holy and righteous. Open our eyes to the consequences of our actions. But thank you that you do not treat us as we deserve. Thank you that you offer us redemption by the blood of Jesus Christ. Amen

17 December

Hoping for peace

The people walking in darkness
    have seen a great light;
on those living in the land of deep darkness
    a light has dawned.
You have enlarged the nation
    and increased their joy;
they rejoice before you
    as people rejoice at the harvest,
as warriors rejoice
    when dividing the plunder.
For as in the day of Midian's defeat,
    you have shattered
the yoke that burdens them,
    the bar across their shoulders,
    the rod of their oppressor.
Every warrior's boot used in battle
    and every garment rolled in blood
will be destined for burning,
    will be fuel for the fire.
For to us a child is born,
    to us a son is given,
    and the government will be on his shoulders.
And he will be called
    Wonderful Counsellor, Mighty God,
    Everlasting Father, Prince of Peace.
Of the greatness of his government and peace
    there will be no end.

> He will reign on David's throne
>   and over his kingdom,
> establishing and upholding it
>   with justice and righteousness
>   from that time on and forever.
> The zeal of the Lord Almighty
>   will accomplish this.
>
> ISAIAH 9:2–7

At this time of year, sometimes the only moment of stillness and reflection in my life comes in a candlelit carol service. The familiar readings, melodies and prayers tether me to the heart of the festivities: a baby boy born to be Saviour of the world.

If you've been to a carol service, it's likely you heard Isaiah 9 read. It is one of the classic Christmas passages, which is why we can be dulled to the astonishing fact that the words were first spoken centuries before the birth of Christ. The tense makes sense in AD but not in BC: 'a child is born… a son is given' (v. 6). Isaiah's belief in God's faithfulness to his promises is boldly expressed in the present tense. In his mind, the baby is as good as arrived.

Of the titles given to the long-awaited king, perhaps the one most heavily laden with hope and expectation is 'Prince of Peace'. I wonder what peace means to you. We often pair it with the word 'quiet' or contrast it with the word 'war'. It speaks of inner tranquillity, contentment and calm. There was more to it in Isaiah's time, though.

The peace the Old Testament people of God hoped for so desperately was multifaceted. First, it involved a secure food supply. What is the best example of a joy-giving situation? A successful harvest (v. 3). In my part of the world, relatively few people other than dieters go to bed hungry. The only time I've seen empty shelves in my local supermarket was shortly after the first coronavirus lockdown, when people rushed to stockpile beans and toilet paper in the event that they had to self-isolate. For those who live without the certainty of a next meal, however, there is no peace to be had. The story is told about how children released from concentration camps after World War II could not sleep without a piece of bread in their hand. For their bodies to relax into the gift of oblivion, they needed the comfort of knowing food would be there when they next needed it.

Second, it meant safety from enemies and, better yet, an end to war altogether. It seems every generation needs to learn for itself that there is nothing grand and glorious in fighting. If you've lived in a war-zone, you'll know all that thrives there is ugliness, trauma, brutality and hardship. Isaiah's prophecy was a picture of hope that one day army boots and bloodied clothing would be chucked on to a giant bonfire. The nations will 'beat their swords into ploughshares and their spears into pruning hooks' (2:4). When the government of the world is on this son's shoulders, peace will reign (9:6).

Third, it meant lasting peace with God. Reading the whole book of Isaiah, rather than just the extracts we dwell on in carol services, shows just how far from peaceful was God's relationship with his people. The people's propensity for evil tried the divine patience to breaking point over and again. It makes for painful reading because the pattern of sin, repent, start again, fail again seems doomed to repeat into infinity. But there's this hope: a Prince of Peace, God's solution.

Our place in the great story of salvation echoes Isaiah's. We too strain our eyes to the horizon, waiting expectantly for deliverance. We live in a world where there is still hunger. Southern Africa faces terrible food shortages largely due to the dire impact of climate change. In Zimbabwe alone 7.7 million people – half the population – were food insecure in the first half of 2020. As I write, there are more than 40 active conflicts across the globe. War is not a thing of the past. There is a key difference, though. Isaiah was right to be confident. The Son was born and, in his life, death and resurrection, he made lasting peace between God and people possible. The boundaries of his kingdom might not extend to the far reaches of the universe yet, but they will. And so we wait. We wait and we hope.

For reflection

Think about what it meant for the Old Testament Jews to wait for a Prince of Peace. As part of Christ's body on earth, how can you bring his peace in the world?

Prayer

Lord, may your peace, which transcends all understanding, guard my heart and my mind in Christ Jesus. Amen

18 December

Hoping for restoration

Strengthen the feeble hands,
    steady the knees that give way;
say to those with fearful hearts,
    'Be strong, do not fear;
your God will come,
    he will come with vengeance;
with divine retribution
    he will come to save you.'

Then will the eyes of the blind be opened
    and the ears of the deaf unstopped.
Then will the lame leap like a deer,
    and the mute tongue shout for joy.
Water will gush forth in the wilderness
    and streams in the desert.
The burning sand will become a pool,
    the thirsty ground bubbling springs.
In the haunts where jackals once lay,
    grass and reeds and papyrus will grow.

And a highway will be there;
    it will be called the Way of Holiness;
    it will be for those who walk on that Way.
The unclean will not journey on it;
    wicked fools will not go about on it.
No lion will be there,
    nor any ravenous beast;
    they will not be found there.

> But only the redeemed will walk there,
>> and those the Lord has rescued will return.
> They will enter Zion with singing;
>> everlasting joy will crown their heads.
> Gladness and joy will overtake them,
>> and sorrow and sighing will flee away.
>
> ISAIAH 35:3–10

I went to boarding school when I was 13. The first couple of years were the most miserable of my life. I spent a lot of time looking for private places to cry – these are few and far between when you share every inch of living space with 500 other teenagers. The showers in the sports hall were usually free (the smell in the changing room was all the confirmation you'd need that there was unlikely to be anyone using them), but after I joined the photography club I had a better spot. The developing room was warm and dark and the chemicals smelled downright pleasant by comparison. If you've ever developed your own photos, you'll know the magic of the process and the strangeness of images on the negatives. Let's look at today's passage first in its negative form and then at the inverse image it creates as the transformation happens.

We don't hope for what we already have. By definition, hope is about future possibilities. By looking at what is hoped for here, we can see a picture of the harsh reality of the present Isaiah spoke into. Although we are years and miles apart, so many of the struggles we have are the same.

Verses 3 and 4 speak of an overwhelming fear, the kind that takes over the body, making knees shake and hands lose their grip. Will God come to save them? Will their enemies be overthrown and receive justice? In the same way that Peter could walk on water when he kept his eyes on Jesus (Matthew 14:22–31), our fear recedes as our faith in God grows stronger.

Verses 5 and 6 describe the most debilitating physical conditions, the ones that took sufferers out of society and isolated them, the ones only a miracle could cure. When the blind could see and the deaf hear, they would know God had come. It was no accident that Jesus healed exactly these conditions. The healing miracles were nothing less than letters across the sky: deliverance has come! Your Saviour is here!

Verses 6 and 7 recall the 40 years of wilderness wandering, when God gave the Israelites water where there was none. Humans can survive a maximum of three days without hydration, so a picture of gushing, bubbling springs is essentially a picture of security. The Covid-19 pandemic showed many wealthy nations' ideas about stability and safety to be illusions. The climate crisis will have escalated by the time you hold this book in your hands, unless we make some drastic changes. Who knows what new war lies around the corner?

Verses 8 to 10 convey a longing for companionship with others in pursuit of holiness – no more wicked fools or unclean idiots. No more dangerous distractions to take them from the Way. This is a heart cry from the people in exile, far from home, among foreigners and their false gods. They hope for a time when they will return to Zion for good, when their joy will be eternal.

Jonathan Bryan was born early and with severe complications after his mother was in a car accident while heavily pregnant. Unable to do anything for himself, everyone assumed his mind was as limited as his body, until his mother was able to help him communicate by directing his eyes to letters on a board. He went on to write an entire book using this painstaking method, *Eye Can Write*, and he has campaigned tirelessly for all children to be given access to education. One of the revelations about Jonathan's inner life, only apparent once he could communicate, was his profound relationship with God. In his book he writes about one of the times he came close to death and his experience of heaven – the presence of Jesus and a whole and healthy body. It was hard for him to return to the realities of his life with its constant and acute pain and frustration. But at his confirmation, these were his words: 'With Jesus as my Saviour, companion and friend, I have lived my hours here with happiness in my spirit and content calm in my soul.' Jonathan inspires me to seek the same contentment while waiting for the image from the negative to appear in full colour.

For reflection

Where do you see the need for restoration in your life, in the lives of those you love and in the world around you? What signs can you see that God is already at work? How can you wait more faithfully, courageously and contentedly for the full restoration in the new heavens and new earth?

Prayer

Lord, you see the whole picture, but sometimes all I can see are dark, blurry shadows. Give me eyes that can take in the beauty of what you are doing here and now. Increase my hope in what you have promised to do. In the precious name of Jesus, Amen

19 December

Hoping for an eternal ruler

'As I looked,
    thrones were set in place,
        and the Ancient of Days took his seat.
His clothing was as white as snow;
    the hair of his head was white like wool.
His throne was flaming with fire,
    and its wheels were all ablaze.
A river of fire was flowing,
    coming out from before him.
Thousands upon thousands attended him;
    ten thousand times ten thousand stood before him.
The court was seated,
    and the books were opened.
'Then I continued to watch because of the boastful words the horn was speaking. I kept looking until the beast was slain and its body destroyed and thrown into the blazing fire. (The other beasts had been stripped of their authority, but were allowed to live for a period of time.)

'In my vision at night I looked, and there before me was one like a son of man, coming with the clouds of heaven. He approached the Ancient of Days and was led into his presence. He was given authority, glory and sovereign power; all nations and peoples of every language worshipped him. His dominion is an everlasting dominion that will not pass away, and his kingdom is one that will never be destroyed.'

DANIEL 7:9–14

Humans were created to need no other ruler but God, but as Israelite society grew more complex and sin made its mark on corporate structures, God's chosen nation requested a king to take charge. Saul was the first to be anointed to the task. He began well but latterly became consumed by jealous rage and focused all his efforts on attempting to assassinate his eventual successor, David.

David is described as a man after God's own heart (1 Samuel 13:14). He is still considered the greatest of Israel's kings and in many ways was the kind of king the people craved. Yet he was a man of violence and lust, and his failures were as numerous as his victories. From then on, Israel and Judah had a succession of terrible, cruel, idolatrous and corrupt monarchs. By the time Daniel, the author of our passage, was taken into Babylonian exile along with vast numbers of his fellow citizens, there was an understandable desperation for good leadership.

Daniel's vision falls into a genre we are largely unfamiliar with in the 21st century: apocalyptic literature. This form of writing is concerned with end times, has a narrative form and involves highly visual, symbolic representations of spiritual ideas and themes. While not intended to be read literally on matters such as hair colour or throne features, today's passage tells us a lot about the kind of ruler Israel longed for and, from a New Testament perspective, about the one we know came to vindicate their hope.

This is a picture that holds together God's rule of his people ('the Ancient of Days') and the people's desire for a human ruler ('one like a son of man'). They are able to rule together, and they unify the world in its worship of them. Under this rule, the main beast is destroyed, though the lesser beasts are allowed to continue living for a while. For those suffering in servitude to a foreign power, far from home, this hope that God would ultimately destroy the great enemy and source of evil must have been a profound comfort. Perhaps it felt like being in a wartime concentration camp but knowing the war was won by your side and liberation was on its way.

One of the most important features of this reign is that it will never end. Transitions of power are notoriously fraught with danger. Even at their best, they are unsettling and always involve losses along with any gains. The Jews lived in hope that one day they would live in an unassailable kingdom, under a ruler whose 'dominion is an everlasting dominion that will not pass away' (v. 14).

For reflection

As followers of Jesus, we are citizens of a kingdom that will never end. In what ways does living under God's rule impact your life day to day? What do you find hardest about waiting for the kingdom to come in all its fullness?

Prayer

Lord God, thank you that you have all authority, glory and sovereign power. I worship you. I submit to your rule over my life. I ask you to help me wait patiently for your kingdom to extend over all the earth. Amen

20 December

Hope deferred

This is what the Lord Almighty, the God of Israel, says to all those I carried into exile from Jerusalem to Babylon: 'Build houses and settle down; plant gardens and eat what they produce. Marry and have sons and daughters; find wives for your sons and give your daughters in marriage, so that they too may have sons and daughters. Increase in number there; do not decrease. Also, seek the peace and prosperity of the city to which I have carried you into exile. Pray to the Lord for it, because if it prospers, you too will prosper.' Yes, this is what the Lord Almighty, the God of Israel, says: 'Do not let the prophets and diviners among you deceive you. Do not listen to the dreams you encourage them to have. They are prophesying lies to you in my name. I have not sent them,' declares the Lord.

This is what the Lord says: 'When seventy years are completed for Babylon, I will come to you and fulfil my good promise to bring you back to this place. For I know the plans I have for you,' declares the Lord, 'plans to prosper you and not to harm you, plans to give you hope and a future. Then you will call on me and come and pray to me, and I will listen to you. You will seek me and find me when you seek me with all your heart. I will be found by you,' declares the Lord, 'and will bring you back from captivity.'

JEREMIAH 29:4–14

Waiting is hard, but in many situations hope is vindicated. In five days, we'll wake up to the joys of Christmas morning. All being well, after nine long months a baby is born. Endless-seeming building projects reach completion. Exam results are posted.

Yet how about those times when we wait, and wait some more, and what we are waiting for never arrives? Those who discover month after month that they haven't conceived a longed-for child. Kate and Gerry McCann hearing nothing about the whereabouts of their daughter for over a decade. The refugee who lives a lifetime in a temporary camp waiting for asylum. As Proverbs 13:12 puts it, 'Hope deferred makes the heart sick.'

My culture, in the southern UK in the early 2020s, is marked by individualism and instant gratification. Choices are made based on immediate results and personal impact. This makes it hard for me to hear the message of Jeremiah to the exiles in Babylon as they would have received it. I have work to do.

You are probably familiar with one particular verse in today's reading: 'For I know the plans I have for you,' declares the Lord, 'plans to prosper you and not to harm you, plans to give you hope and a future' (v. 11). It is the kind of verse that gets printed on cards and made into needlepoint cushions, bookmarks and fridge magnets.

When we read it in its wider setting, however, it doesn't say quite what we'd like it to. It isn't on the scale we thought. It isn't a marble – it's a planet. Any comfort we take from applying it to our own specific angst is false because it is not promising a better job or a cancer-free biopsy. But the comfort it does hold out is profound – life-changing, even.

The first thing to notice is that this message has a specific target audience: 'all those I carried into exile' (v. 4). It is written to a collective, not an individual, and it is written for people in a particular situation. They are under the Lord's discipline, experiencing the consequences of long-term, systematic disobedience. The punishment is harsh and strikes at the heart of their identity as a people set apart and blessed by God.

God is, was and will be merciful, patient and forgiving, so this is a message containing hope. God's plans are for good. He does not want to harm them, but to bring them back to him and to give them a future. Catch this, though: this is not a future within the lifetimes of the majority of those to whom the message was delivered. The return to the promised land would not happen for a further 70 years (v. 10). This is where we have to make a cultural jump out of our short-termist individualism. The fact that God hadn't given up on their nation was the best news. The fact that future generations would live once again in the promised land was cause for celebration. The reminder that God's ultimate concern was for a restored relationship with his people enabled them to focus on what they could do to learn the lessons of exile.

For reflection

How are you experiencing 'hope deferred' at the moment? What do you think God might be saying to you about your focus in this time of waiting? How can the bigger story of salvation and restoration bring you comfort?

Prayer

Lord God, may the words of the psalmist be true for me today: 'I wait for the Lord, my whole being waits, and in his word I put my hope' (Psalm 130:5).

God among us

I N OUR BIBLES, the last book of the Old Testament is Malachi and then we turn a page and there we are in the gospel of Matthew. Between the two were 500 years of silence: 25 generations were born, lived and died waiting for a messiah.

And then, distant rumblings became a roar. The waiting was over. This time was now.

An angel visited a young, unmarried girl and, soon after, she conceived a child by the Holy Spirit. Her baby was born in Bethlehem as the prophecy had foretold. A heavenly host alerted local shepherds, and wise men from the east followed the night sky to his side. The baby's arrival was not well received by the reigning monarch, Herod, who unleashed a terrible slaughter of male infants in the vain attempt to eliminate his competition. Jesus escaped, a refugee in Egypt with his mother, Mary, and her husband Joseph. The rest, as they say, is history.

If ever a man could be said to bear the weight of the world on his shoulders, it was Jesus. Jesus was strong enough to bear the weight, because in the greatest mystery of all time, he was both man and God. This coming week, we'll be considering the ways he met and continues to meet the expectations on him and the needs of a broken humanity.

21 December

Light of the world

In him was life, and that life was the light of all mankind.
The light shines in the darkness, and the darkness has not
overcome it.

There was a man sent from God whose name was John.
He came as a witness to testify concerning that light, so that
through him all might believe. He himself was not the light;
he came only as a witness to the light.

The true light that gives light to everyone was coming
into the world. He was in the world, and though the world
was made through him, the world did not recognise him.
He came to that which was his own, but his own did not
receive him. Yet to all who did receive him, to those who
believed in his name, he gave the right to become children
of God – children born not of natural descent, nor of human
decision or a husband's will, but born of God.

JOHN 1:4–13

On my part of the globe, today is the darkest day of the year, the
moment the north pole is furthest from the sun. As a glass-half-full
kind of girl, I like to think of it as the day when we can start to look
forward to more light, but in truth there are a lot of long nights to
come. However much I try to cheer myself with candles, fairy lights
and fireside cups of tea, given the option I'd happily migrate to sunnier
climes and skip winter altogether.

Darkness and light are powerful metaphors and appear often in
biblical literature. Like oil and water, they cannot mix. Unlike hot and

cold, they do not exert an equal influence on the other. They are not neutral: darkness has almost universally negative connotations and light the converse.

When the Bible speaks of people living in darkness, it tells us they are moving through life without God. In the dark they have no sense of direction and they stumble (John 11:10). They cannot see and so lack understanding (Romans 1:21). They feel free to behave in terrible ways, thinking what they do is hidden and secret: 'People loved darkness instead of light because their deeds were evil. Everyone who does evil hates the light, and will not come into the light for fear that their deeds will be exposed' (John 3:19–20). Around this time of year, many companies hold office parties. These occasions are notorious for the foolish behaviour, unprofessional gossip and sordid liaisons that can happen as the night progresses and the alcohol flows. The same event held at midday would have an entirely different feel.

Darkness is Satan's realm, grave-like and hopeless, and Jesus is 'the true light' (v. 9). As he spoke light into being at the dawn of creation, so at his birth as a human baby he brought a new reality into being. His arrival shone rays of hope and life into the world.

All it takes to dispel darkness is one flickering match. When John says, 'The light shines in the darkness, and the darkness has not overcome it' (v. 5), he means nothing less than that Jesus has defeated the great enemy of goodness, the devil.

The original New Testament Greek word for overcome, *katelaben*, also carries the meaning 'to understand'. The light is for everyone (vv. 4, 9), but for some it didn't bring clarity, only more confusion and an urge to flee into the shadows. For now, there's a choice: live in the light or remain in the dark. Will we receive him? Will we believe in his name?

For reflection

The Jewish teenage diarist Anne Frank wrote, 'Look at how a single candle can both defy and define the darkness.' If you are able, light a candle and turn off any lights in the room. Let your mind rest on the idea of Jesus as the light of the world.

Prayer

Jesus, you are the light of the world – the source of life and the bringer of hope and clarity. On this dark December day, I turn my face towards you. I thank you for coming into this world and scattering the darkness. Amen

22 December

One of us

Therefore, since we have a great high priest who has ascended into heaven, Jesus the Son of God, let us hold firmly to the faith we profess. For we do not have a high priest who is unable to feel sympathy for our weaknesses, but we have one who has been tempted in every way, just as we are – yet he did not sin. Let us then approach God's throne of grace with confidence, so that we may receive mercy and find grace to help us in our time of need...

During the days of Jesus' life on earth, he offered up prayers and petitions with fervent cries and tears to the one who could save him from death, and he was heard because of his reverent submission. Son though he was, he learned obedience from what he suffered and, once made perfect, he became the source of eternal salvation for all who obey him and was designated by God to be high priest in the order of Melchizedek.

HEBREWS 4:14–16; 5:7–10

In the town where I learnt to drive, there were three driving examiners. According to urban legend, two of them were fine, but if you had the third and were under 21, you were toast; you might as well book your second test on the spot. As the story went, this examiner had lost his precious daughter in a car accident. The driver of the other car? You guessed it – a 20-year-old with a brand-new driving licence. As we left the test centre to walk to the car, the examiner told me his name and that was it. Whether or not the story had any truth, my nerves gave out and it was downhill from there.

That is a trivial example of the fact that everyone who has power over us in any way is a human, with human prejudices, blind spots, foibles and limitations. I happen to know three judges. While they are more impressive, wise and intelligent than most of us could dream of being, up close, they are still pretty ordinary. There's something a bit scary about that.

There are lots of metaphors in the Bible to help us understand who Jesus was, and how his relationship to us works. He called himself the good shepherd, the bread of life, the way, the truth and the life and the Son of God. Here he is described by the writer of Hebrews as 'a great high priest'.

High priests served as intermediaries between worshippers and God. They offered sacrifices on behalf of sinners and interceded for them. They had enormous spiritual and political power under the old covenant.

To have Jesus as our high priest means we can relax. Things are going to be okay for us, because Jesus was one of us. He knows from the inside how hard it is to experience life's great and dangerous temptations. He's walked the proverbial mile in the moccasins. He's the boss who's done the time on the shop floor.

Not only that, but he experienced acute suffering on the night he wrestled with God in Gethsemane: 'He offered up prayers and petitions with fervent cries and tears to the one who could save him from death' (5:7). The tears were genuine. Jesus, though God, was not spared the most painful human experience possible and, as a result, we know he understands the very depths of what we might face.

A couple of things to mention before we finish. Did you catch the inference that Jesus was anything less than flawless – 'once made perfect' (5:9). Perfect in this sentence refers to the idea of completion or accomplishment. It was the crucifixion that made him the 'source of eternal salvation for all who obey him', so until he'd been to the cross, his work was unfinished.

And Melchizedek: who was he? Well, other than Melchizedek, all priests were from the tribe of Levi and there for the people of Israel. This meant the role came with the lineage rather than through individual calling or personal piety and because of that, there were a fair few terrible priests around, even high priests. Melchizedek appears in Genesis 14, blessing Abram after a battle with Sodom. He's referred to as 'priest of God Most High' as well as the king of Salem. Not only is he not a Levite, but he's not even one of the chosen nation. For Jesus to be 'in the order of Melchizedek' tells us that he is righteous and worthy and that he's a priest for all nations, not just Israel.

For reflection

What qualities would you hope for in a person who had power over an important aspect of your life? How does Jesus' humanity make him a perfect high priest?

Prayer

Lord God, I come to you, the judge of all, and to Jesus, the mediator of a new covenant, and to the Holy Spirit, giver of new life, in confidence because of what you have done for me. Help me to be properly thankful and to worship you with reverence and awe. Amen

23 December

God revealed

The Son is the image of the invisible God, the firstborn over all creation. For in him all things were created: things in heaven and on earth, visible and invisible, whether thrones or powers or rulers or authorities; all things have been created through him and for him. He is before all things, and in him all things hold together. And he is the head of the body, the church; he is the beginning and the firstborn from among the dead, so that in everything he might have the supremacy.

COLOSSIANS 1:15–18

Have you ever lived for a period of time in a country where you don't speak the language? There can be people all around you, but the loneliness of an inability to understand or be understood is crushing. There may be signs on every street corner, but you can still get lost. However much you smile, gesticulate or draw passers-by into impromptu games of Pictionary, there's an impermeable barrier to communication. What you need is a translator.

All through the Old Testament, God went to extraordinary lengths to communicate with people. He spoke, he made bushes burn, he inscribed stone tablets, he parted water and he planted dreams and visions. He endowed creation with majesty, beauty and a fearsome wildness that spoke of his character. He anointed prophets as his mouthpieces and raised up priests to direct honouring worship. All the time, though, the chasm between God and humanity seemed to widen. So God took it upon himself to close the gap. He became one of us, so we could see him and hear him. Jesus was God translated: 'the image of the invisible God' (v. 15).

The implications of God being born a human are enormous. For today, let's just focus on what this part of Paul's letter to the early church in Colossae tells us: quite enough for us to get our heads around!

What strikes me most strongly is how the incarnation is a resounding affirmation of the physical creation. The Colossian church had been infiltrated by those who believed matter was inherently unspiritual. It led to two equally unfortunate extremes: harsh treatment of the body and unrestrained sensual indulgence (2:23). The heresies of dualism and Gnosticism continue to lurk around today. Hundreds of worship songs include lyrics about being lifted away to a heavenly home and focusing only on Jesus (as 'the things of earth grow strangely dim'); very few speak of our part in Jesus' ongoing redemption of *all things* (Romans 8:20–21). Creation was made 'through him and for him' (v. 16). Our treatment of our own physical bodies and the world around us has everything to do with the degree to which we love and respect the creator of all things.

Another implication is that Jesus was God made visible, meaning *he could be seen*! We are used to this idea, so it may sound obvious, but it is actually mind-blowing. The eternal, all-powerful, all-knowing, ineffable God was, for a short while, small enough to be cradled in a person's embrace.

In Luke 2 there is a moving account of an elderly man named Simeon who, through the Holy Spirit, knew the Messiah would come in his lifetime. Taking Jesus in his arms, he prayed, 'Sovereign Lord, as you have promised, you may now dismiss your servant in peace. For my eyes have seen your salvation, which you have prepared in the sight of all nations' (vv. 29–31).

It may have been over 2,000 years ago, but the gift of God made visible continues to bless believers today. Despite our limited imaginations, we can encounter the person of Jesus through the accounts of the gospel writers Matthew, Mark, Luke and John. And one day we'll meet face to face, with joyful cries of recognition.

For reflection

Take your imagination to the place and time of Jesus' birth. What can you see? Hear? Smell? Touch? Where are you in this picture? Move closer to the baby. Reach out your arms and pick him up. What does it feel like to be holding him? What thoughts go through your mind as you look at him, feel his warmth and his weight, smell that newborn fragrance and hear his snuffles?

Prayer

Oh Lord, thank you for taking on flesh and dwelling among your people for a time. Thank you that you were fully human as well as fully God. Help me grasp more of what that means. Amen

24 December

Love in human form

'As the Father has loved me, so have I loved you. Now remain in my love. If you keep my commands, you will remain in my love, just as I have kept my Father's commands and remain in his love. I have told you this so that my joy may be in you and that your joy may be complete. My command is this: love each other as I have loved you. Greater love has no one than this: to lay down one's life for one's friends. You are my friends if you do what I command. I no longer call you servants, because a servant does not know his master's business. Instead, I have called you friends, for everything that I learned from my Father I have made known to you. You did not choose me, but I chose you and appointed you so that you might go and bear fruit – fruit that will last – and so that whatever you ask in my name the Father will give you. This is my command: love each other.'
JOHN 15:9–17

Christmas Eve has come! I wonder what the day holds for you? Mine will be dominated by food prep – stuffing the turkey, peeling the spuds and carrots, and making the brandy butter and, in a nod to the Americans in the family, a pecan pie. There will be last-minute pressie wrapping, a stocking-hanging ceremony, a tipple by the fire. We are pretty traditional when it comes to Christmas. Although I often find the day tiring and a bit stressful, hosting a proper celebration tomorrow is for me a matter of expressing love. I want every mouthful of festive food and every gift unwrapped to say, 'You are loved.' That's the intention, anyway. We're a normal family, and it goes wrong just as much as it goes right.

As humans we are primarily fuelled by love. Without it we shrivel. We go to crazy lengths to find it. We bask in its warmth and flourish in its glow. Love is the most common theme in our music, art and literature, mostly of the romantic sort, but also love within families and friendships and even towards pets, places and possessions.

So much of the brokenness in our world comes down to the fact that love is so often misunderstood, withheld or twisted out of shape. The distortion of love is not a new thing, but different eras have their own particular dysfunctional tendencies. In the 21st century in my part of the world, we associate love with feelings, sex and the ideas of acceptance and tolerance. Today's love has very little to do with love as the Bible portrays it. And it leaves us hungry and dissatisfied.

If our brokenness is at root a lack of love, in Jesus came healing: eternal, gracious, endless love. The truest form of love is God himself. In becoming human, God translated love into a form we could understand.

These words of Jesus in John 15 give us a glimpse into how love works within the Trinity. Our task is to mirror what we see, in our interactions with God and with each other. As we do this, we will experience joy – the same joy Jesus has in his relationship with God (v. 11).

Love within the Trinity is entwined with obedience. 'I have kept my Father's commands,' says Jesus, 'and remain in his love' (v. 10). And how do we remain in his love? By keeping his commands. This association might strike us as uncomfortable or even a bit odd at first. We probably wouldn't have thought to pair the two words on our own. But what are we saying when we choose to keep God's commands? We are saying we trust him to know what is best. We are saying we prioritise our relationship with him over our own agendas. We are saying we will love in what we do and not just what we say.

Love within the Trinity could not be more of a contrast to love 'as seen on TV' – cheap, temporary, transactional and brazenly selfish. Divine love is demanding and costly. It took Jesus to the cross. It asks us for everything we have and more.

Love within the Trinity does not just bless the Trinity – it overflows, blessing and embracing all who come close. The more we understand and experience the love God has for us, the greater our love becomes for others, regardless of how loveable they might be in worldly terms. 'Love each other as I have loved you' (v. 12) is ultimately a command to pour ourselves out for others, as Christ has poured himself out for us. The seemingly impossible can be done because he has done it first and shown us how.

For reflection

Sit quietly for as long as you can. Focus your mind on the love of God as expressed in the birth of Jesus. This love is for you.

Prayer

> *Love divine, all loves excelling,*
> *Joy of heaven to earth come down,*
> *Fix in us thy humble dwelling,*
> *All thy faithful mercies crown.*
> *Jesus, thou art all compassion,*
> *Pure, unbounded love thou art;*
> *Visit us with thy salvation,*
> *Enter every trembling heart. (Charles Wesley)*
> *Amen*

25 December

For the least, the last and the lost

> While they were there, the time came for the baby to be born, and she gave birth to her firstborn, a son. She wrapped him in cloths and placed him in a manger, because there was no guest room available for them.
>
> And there were shepherds living out in the fields near by, keeping watch over their flocks at night. An angel of the Lord appeared to them, and the glory of the Lord shone around them, and they were terrified. But the angel said to them, 'Do not be afraid. I bring you good news that will cause great joy for all the people. Today in the town of David a Saviour has been born to you; he is the Messiah, the Lord.'
>
> LUKE 2:6–11

Happy Christmas! Wherever you are and whatever you are doing, I pray you will know the presence of Emmanuel, God with you.

A couple of years ago I got a tin of lateral-thinking puzzles in my stocking (Father Christmas delivers to the adults in our house too). Here is one of them: a man is driving his son to school when they are involved in a terrible accident. By the time the first responders arrive, only the son is alive. He's rushed to hospital in an ambulance. The first doctor to see him takes one look at his face and exclaims in shock, 'That's my son!' Who is the doctor?

To my shame, it took me several wrong and increasingly outlandish suggestions before I arrived at the right answer: the doctor was his mother. The reason this is a puzzle at all is because many of us, me apparently included, have an unconscious bias. The first female doctor in the UK was Elizabeth Garrett Anderson, licensed in 1865, and 45 per cent of doctors are now women, so the assumption exposed by this mind game must run pretty deep.

Expectations and hopes for a coming Messiah had been building for an extremely long time by the birth of Jesus. Some of these were formed from prophecies, such as the ones we've been looking at. Others reflected the longings of a people who'd been mistreated by a succession of stronger political powers, latterly the Roman empire. And some came from sin-warped ideas of leadership and strength, many of which persist today. In the school playground, popularity is conferred on those with the glossiest hair, the clearest skin and the newest and most expensive kit. In adult life little changes.

The life of Jesus, from conception to resurrection, was a signpost to God's character and priorities. Given how different these were from what the majority were looking for, many people at the time were not able to see Jesus for who he was. This has remained true to this day and especially so in those places in the world most endowed with health, wealth and individual freedoms.

The gospel writers were highly selective in the details they chose to include in their accounts. We are supposed to pay careful attention and catch the significance of what we find there. When Luke tells us Jesus was laid in a manger because there was no guest room, what does he want us to hear? God incarnate had not come to be part of the ruling elite. He had been born to an ordinary young girl in sur-roundings more appropriate for animals than humans. The prophets had conveyed God's heart for the poor, the displaced and the down-trodden with uncompromising clarity. Jesus' birthplace was just one of the confirmations that God's heart had not changed.

Then we have the first public birth announcement, given in the middle of the night in far-flung fields to a group of shepherds. Shepherds had a similar status to today's bin collectors or road maintenance crews. They fulfilled an important service but operated somewhat at the margins, kept unsociable hours and could be a bit whiffy, through no fault of their own. This was 'good news that will cause great joy for all the people' (v. 10), but the shepherds were the first recipients. The angel of the Lord could have chosen anyone to tell first and *he chose them*.

Jesus was a gift to the world, but most especially to the least, the last and the lost. For those of us who don't fall into those categories, there are challenges if we can hear them. God asks us to love him above all else – to worship him and him only. Can we hold our power, position and possessions lightly? Where our treasure is, there we'll find our hearts, so what do we treasure?

And as followers of Christ, how do our lives reflect his priorities? What are we doing, as individuals, in our church families and as part of the global church, to reach out with love to the last, the least and the lost?

For reflection

What do you think might have changed for the shepherds after this angelic encounter?

Prayer

Father God, I know when I come to you I am often blinded by my own assumptions, prejudices and cultural conditioning. Open my eyes to the truth of who you are. Show me your heart. Help me to experience the joy of your salvation. Amen

26 December

The defeat of death

If only for this life we have hope in Christ, we are of all people most to be pitied.

But Christ has indeed been raised from the dead, the firstfruits of those who have fallen asleep. For since death came through a man, the resurrection of the dead comes also through a man. For as in Adam all die, so in Christ all will be made alive. But each in turn: Christ, the firstfruits; then, when he comes, those who belong to him. Then the end will come, when he hands over the kingdom to God the Father after he has destroyed all dominion, authority and power. For he must reign until he has put all his enemies under his feet. The last enemy to be destroyed is death.

1 CORINTHIANS 15:19–26

Death: the heart stops, blood stops flowing, no oxygen replenishes the cells, the brain and other organs shut down. The person has left the body, and the body will soon return to the ground – dust to dust, ashes to ashes.

Something in us knows that death is wrong. It wasn't part of the original plan but was brought into the system by Adam (v. 21) and, of all the ways we suffer, it causes the most pain. We are afraid of it, outraged by it, angry with it. Paul is right to call it our 'enemy' (v. 26).

There are some interesting examples of ways people have tried to fight back. The Cryonics Institute claims to 'offer hope' to those with enough money to pay for their bodies to be preserved with liquid nitrogen until scientists figure out a reanimation technique. On their website they proclaim, 'Cryonics is a visionary concept that holds out the promise of a second chance at life – with renewed health, vitality and youth.'

The small town of Otsuchi in northern Japan lost 2,000 residents in the tsunami of 2011. A survivor set up a phone booth in his garden, and now thousands come to speak to their lost loved ones over its disconnected line. I understand this impulse so well, as I'm sure anyone who has been bereaved does. But I do not believe the wind would carry my voice to its intended recipient, so a visit to the booth would not comfort me.

The ancient Egyptians mummified bodies to keep them intact for transportation to the afterlife. The powerful and wealthy were packed into pyramids with possessions, pets and even spouses and servants. Their hope was not 'only for this life', but its source was the limits of their own imaginations: mere longing for wish fulfilment.

However we fight it, the best we can do is put off the evil hour. Death comes for us all eventually, even after the life, death and resurrection of Jesus. So how did Jesus defeat death? What is the hope he offers us?

First, the hope is concrete and earthy. When Jesus died, he was *actually dead* – no heartbeat, no blood flow, no oxygen, no brain activity. His resurrection body was an *actual body*. He could be touched, he ate food, he walked and talked and he embraced his friends. He 'has indeed been raised from the dead' (v. 20) and remains alive to this day and forever more.

Second, however final it seems, God's perspective on death is that it is a temporary state. The dead 'have fallen asleep' (v. 20) and those who belong to Christ will be woken 'when he comes' (v. 23). When a Christian we love dies, we grieve because we are separated from them. The parting is painful, and the loss is real and immediate. Jesus himself wept when Lazarus died, knowing full well he would be alive again in a matter of hours (see John 11). But the sorrow will be followed by the most joyous reunions, of that we can be confident. If we don't believe that, as Paul says, we are to be pitied (v. 19).

Third, although death is still very much part of life now, one day it won't be. Paul uses both the past and the future tenses here. Christ has been raised from the dead. This happened, and it can give us confidence as we wait. For now, the enemies of God have 'dominion, authority and power' (v. 24), but the time is coming when death itself will meet its end.

For reflection

How do you feel about your own death? What difference does being a Christian make to your thoughts about dying? How confident are you that there is life beyond the grave?

Prayer

Lord Jesus, you became human knowing you would be experiencing the worst of what that means – death itself. Thank you that you came through death to life and in doing so have given us hope for what is to come. Help me hold on to your promise that those who love you will be raised to life again, in your kingdom which will never end. Amen

27 December

The gift of life

Therefore Jesus said again, 'Very truly I tell you, I am the gate for the sheep. All who have come before me are thieves and robbers, but the sheep have not listened to them. I am the gate; whoever enters through me will be saved. They will come in and go out, and find pasture. The thief comes only to steal and kill and destroy; I have come that they may have life, and have it to the full.

'I am the good shepherd. The good shepherd lays down his life for the sheep. The hired hand is not the shepherd and does not own the sheep. So when he sees the wolf coming, he abandons the sheep and runs away. Then the wolf attacks the flock and scatters it. The man runs away because he is a hired hand and cares nothing for the sheep.

'I am the good shepherd; I know my sheep and my sheep know me – just as the Father knows me and I know the Father – and I lay down my life for the sheep.'

JOHN 10:7–15

Jesus has saved us from death, but what did he save us *for*? The answer is deceptively simple: life. But what kind of life? As anyone who has had depression, worked years in a boring job, been locked in an unhappy marriage or suffered from a chronic medical condition will testify, life can sometimes bear little resemblance to living.

To fully understand this teaching of Jesus in John 10, we need to back up a bit. It follows an incident which at first seems wholly joyful. Jesus and his disciples encountered a man born blind and reduced to begging for survival, knowing full well his community suspected his infirmity was his fault or his parents'. Jesus first told him his blindness had nothing to do with sin; rather, it 'happened so that the works of God might be displayed in him' (John 9:3). In a few short moments, his greatest shame was transformed into something that could glorify the Almighty God!

The man's dignity thus restored, Jesus then rubbed mud on the man's eyes and gave him back his sight too. What an amazing and wonderful thing to happen – or so you'd think. The Pharisees, whose name meant literally 'separated ones', considered it an outrage. Jesus had performed his miracle on the sabbath, flouting religious laws. Pharisees loved religious laws and enforced them with tyrannical glee. They had set themselves up as a forbidding gateway to God and it is to them Jesus addresses himself in our passage today.

It isn't just Jews from the ancient Near East who falsely believed following God meant following every rule in a library of lawbooks. Many today associate Christianity with restriction, inhibition and a curtailing of fun and the freedom to choose whatever feels good at the time, and on that basis they walk away without a backward glance. But Jesus didn't save us from death for a barely lived life; he saved us for life 'to the full' (v. 10).

What is this fullest of all possible lives, and how do we find it? Jesus said it is all about him. As the gate, he is the entry point – the way in. Life through him is both secure (once in, you are 'saved') and free ('they will come in and go out'). That there is a gate at all is anathema to modern sensibilities. Current orthodoxy frowns upon the concept of ins and outs and prefers to picture us all in one big happy meadow. But there is a thief who ruins that picture. You can't live life to the full when you are vulnerable to theft, murder and destruction (v. 10). The gate is open for anyone who desires to enter. Jesus has given us access to God, in whose 'presence is fullness of joy' (Psalm 16:11, KJV).

He is also 'the good shepherd'. Life to the full is lived in a flock looked after by a shepherd who would (did) do everything to keep you safe.

This shepherd knows you and can be known by you. It is a relationship that begins now, continues for eternity and is the source of the greatest fulfilment, meaning and purpose anyone could imagine.

For reflection

Are you more prone to believe the lie that a full life can be found in pursuing the widest range of experiences and possessions you can or the lie that you can find it in religious piety and self-denial? How have you experienced the truth – that Jesus is at the centre of our search?

Prayer

Lord, I want to live – really live. Thank you that you have given me the gift of life. Thank you for the joy, security and fulfilment I can find in your presence. Amen

Redeemed life

I MET MY HUSBAND SHAWN IN CANADA, where we were both doing postgraduate studies. He is American and I am English. Our first plan was to stay in Vancouver, which we loved, but after a year of marriage we decided we'd like to live close to at least one side of the family, and we moved to the UK. Shawn first had a work permit, which he then upgraded to permanent leave to remain. We were tempted to leave it at that – applying for citizenship was expensive and time-consuming and we felt it wouldn't make much of a difference. In all honesty, this thinking was probably reflective of a certain ambivalence towards our country of residence. We weren't ready to go all in and commit.

A few years down the line and he made the jump. He officially belongs now – it is a matter of identity. He has a say in choosing leaders, must obey the laws and pay taxes and can rely on the state for health care and legal protection. However, the degree to which he participates and integrates into British society is up to him.

When Shawn lived in the UK legally but not as a citizen, he could be compared to the person who does religious activities like going to church, tithing money and reading the Bible, but has no relationship with Jesus. When he became a citizen, he was like the person who has believed in Jesus and entered the kingdom of God. As he has integrated more and more into English society, he is like the person who is inhabiting their identity as a child of God, living more and more in line with who God has declared them to be.

We officially left Advent on 24 December, but the eagle-eyed among you will have spotted that we kept going after Christmas and there are a few pages left in this book. We are together until 6 January, I'm glad to say, so there is time for us to explore more of what it means to live the redeemed life in Christ.

28 December

Peace with God

For Christ's love compels us, because we are convinced that one died for all, and therefore all died. And he died for all, that those who live should no longer live for themselves but for him who died for them and was raised again.

So from now on we regard no one from a worldly point of view. Though we once regarded Christ in this way, we do so no longer. Therefore, if anyone is in Christ, the new creation has come: the old has gone, the new is here! All this is from God, who reconciled us to himself through Christ and gave us the ministry of reconciliation: that God was reconciling the world to himself in Christ, not counting people's sins against them. And he has committed to us the message of reconciliation. We are therefore Christ's ambassadors, as though God were making his appeal through us. We implore you on Christ's behalf: be reconciled to God. God made him who had no sin to be sin for us, so that in him we might become the righteousness of God.

2 CORINTHIANS 5:14–21

Are you an owner of one of the UK's 10 million dogs? If so, I wonder how your pooch behaved over Christmas. Canine temptations abound at this time of year: the postman comes to the door more often, extra pairs of chewy shoes sit around in the hallway, juicy joints of meat are left on kitchen surfaces, bins overflow with interesting rubbish – there are so many exciting ways to get into trouble.

Dogs know when they have done something they shouldn't have and give every appearance of shame on being caught out – droopy eyes, cowering posture, tail between the legs. Scientists say, though, that this show of contrition is actually fear driven and an attempt to avoid punishment.

There are plenty of differences between humans and dogs, but sometimes the dynamic I have described plays out in our relationship with God. We mess up, depressingly often, and then we do a good impression of being really sorry, while actually just wanting to avoid the punishment we instinctively feel is coming our way. We need a new paradigm – a different perspective.

Jesus' life, death and resurrection changed everything. The damage caused by what the Bible calls 'sin' is first and foremost inflicted on God. In Jesus, God absorbed the damage and its consequences on our relationship with him, and what is on offer is a lasting peace. And living in peace with God is transformative. It fundamentally changes our purpose and our identity.

There are a range of purposes that drive people, including survival, wealth, excellence, acceptance and connection. We are all hungry for a narrative that takes the disparate elements of our lives and shapes them into a coherent whole. In this letter to the Corinthian church, Paul is clear: if we are in Christ, we are to live for him (v. 15), becoming his ambassadors to the world (v. 20) and calling everyone to be reconciled to God as we are (v. 19).

Paul also urges his readers not to see Christ, themselves or each other in a worldly way anymore. What is this 'worldly point of view' (v. 16)? Look at the commentary on those braving the red carpet at the Oscars: for the women the focus is on what they are wearing, who they are dating and the size and shape of their bodies. For the men, the interest seems to be in how much they earn, the success of the films they have been in and the beauty and age of their arm candy. From this information they are brutally rated and categorised. We may never find our worth so publicly weighed in these terms, but what we have and how we look does matter to some people. It doesn't matter a jot to God, though. He has given us an identity that supersedes any other factor. It is not just that we have been forgiven our sins; we are entirely new creations (v. 17).

The peace we have with God changes who we are and how and why we do what we do. It may take us time to absorb the full implications of our altered reality, but the sooner we do, the better our lives will be.

For reflection

How can it be that 'God has reconciled us to himself' (v. 18) and yet we still need to 'be reconciled to God' (v. 20)? Why do you think God has created a world in which people have the genuine option of rejecting him?

Prayer

Lord God, thank you that through Jesus you have made me righteous. For all the ways I harm our relationship every day, you never walk away. Help me live as the new creation you have made me, to live in the truth of who I am now, in you. Amen

29 December

Restoring creation

I consider that our present sufferings are not worth
comparing with the glory that will be revealed in us. For
the creation waits in eager expectation for the children
of God to be revealed. For the creation was subjected
to frustration, not by its own choice, but by the will of
the one who subjected it, in hope that the creation itself
will be liberated from its bondage to decay and brought
into the freedom and glory of the children of God.
  We know that the whole creation has been groaning as
in the pains of childbirth right up to the present time. Not
only so, but we ourselves, who have the firstfruits of the
Spirit, groan inwardly as we wait eagerly for our adoption
to sonship, the redemption of our bodies. For in this hope
we were saved. But hope that is seen is no hope at all. Who
hopes for what they already have? But if we hope for what
we do not yet have, we wait for it patiently.
ROMANS 8:18–25

When we read Romans 8, we often zero in on what it says about
humanity – *our* sufferings, *our* hope for freedom and glory. But this
is only part of the picture: 'The creation waits in eager expectation'
(v. 19); 'The creation was subjected to frustration' (v. 20); 'The creation
itself will be liberated' (v. 21); 'The *whole* creation has been groaning'
(v. 22, italics mine).

Paul was writing during what is known as the Holocene era – around
12,000 years of climate stability which enabled humans to invent agri-
culture, settle down and develop great civilisations. But even then,

some seasons the rain didn't come, or too much came and there were floods. Disease struck herds and blighted crops. Species were over-hunted and became extinct. Creation has suffered along with humanity ever since the fall.

But we are in new territory now. Since the 1950s, the scale of human impact has tipped us into a whole other geological epoch, known as the Anthropocene. We have put Earth's life-giving systems under intolerable stress. Our burning of fossil fuels has led to an unprecedented concentration of carbon dioxide in the atmosphere (the safe limit is 350 parts per million; we are at 400 and rising). This is leading to a hotter, drier climate and rising sea levels. We have put more than double the safe level of toxic, synthetic fertilisers into our soil. Since 1970 the number of mammals, birds, reptiles, amphibians and fish has fallen by half.

In looking for a metaphor to express the kind of agony creation experiences, Paul reached for labour. Pretty much anyone who has given birth will tell you the 'pangs of childbirth' are a whole other world of pain. I have had two children. Before my first, I was all about my birth plan and how I would breathe through the contractions while listening to worship music and hopping in and out of a birthing pool. When it came to my second, I was screeching for an epidural the minute I got through the door.

God hears the groaning of creation, and he cares. His love extends to all he has made. His good intentions for redemption and eternal flourishing are for everything, not just people. As Christians we do not have to accept the narrative that the catastrophic abuse of the planet will inevitably lead to its destruction. Yes, there is 'present suffering', but there is also an 'eager expectation' for a coming glory.

As we wait for the fulfilment of all God has in store, we have work to do to care for, honour and restore this beautiful, hurting world in his name. It has lasting value to its maker and what matters to him should matter to us.

For reflection

How can you as an individual, a family and a church work for the restoration of creation for the glory of God?

Prayer

Lord God, this is your world and you love it. The mountains, oceans, plants and creatures give you joy and reflect your glory. Thank you that you made everything to flourish in your great shalom. I am sorry for the ways I have harmed or neglected your creation. Please forgive me and show me how to live in a way that honours you. Amen

30 December

Belonging and love

For just as each of us has one body with many members, and these members do not all have the same function, so in Christ we, though many, form one body, and each member belongs to all the others...

Love must be sincere. Hate what is evil; cling to what is good. Be devoted to one another in love. Honour one another above yourselves. Never be lacking in zeal, but keep your spiritual fervour, serving the Lord. Be joyful in hope, patient in affliction, faithful in prayer. Share with the Lord's people who are in need. Practise hospitality.

Bless those who persecute you; bless and do not curse. Rejoice with those who rejoice; mourn with those who mourn. Live in harmony with one another. Do not be proud, but be willing to associate with people of low position. Do not be conceited.

Do not repay anyone evil for evil. Be careful to do what is right in the eyes of everyone. If it is possible, as far as it depends on you, live at peace with everyone.

ROMANS 12:4–5, 9–18

I grew up in a Christian family. When I was three years old, my dad was ordained in the Anglican church, but after he'd done his curacy (for all you non-Anglicans out there, this is a training post), instead of becoming a vicar, he and my mum pioneered a Christian conservation charity, A Rocha, in southern Portugal. For the rest of my childhood, church looked like an ever-changing gathering of the field study centre community, usually out on the grass under the rubber tree. On our occasional visits back to England, we'd visit a number of churches which supported the charity, giving me a series of shallow impressions of what a more standard set-up looked like. I wasn't impressed, and quietly and rather grandiosely decided I would consider myself part of 'the worldwide church' but you wouldn't catch me darkening the doors of a specific, localised congregation. The joke's on me: I ended up married to a vicar, and I never miss a Sunday. Nor would I want to. I have become a passionate believer in this most ingenious of God's ideas.

The story of the Old Testament revolves around a chosen nation, created by God and blessed with his presence and favour. As far as us Gentiles go, one of the best Christmas presents was an invitation. Membership to this exclusive group was opened up to any who trusted in Christ to save them. Hurray – we're in! Belonging is a fundamental human need, and God has designed it so that everyone who loves him has a place where they are needed, welcomed, safe and accepted for all eternity.

But here's the flip side: you belong to Christ? You belong to everyone else who does, too. Our redeemed lives are lived in the community of our fellow redeemed. And while we wait for our full heavenly transformation, we remain pretty difficult, and so does everyone else. It seemed Paul had no illusions that peace with some people was even feasible ('If it is possible, as far as it depends on you', v. 18). It would be far less stressful to opt out and get some good one-on-one time with God, perhaps in some beautiful, remote countryside.

But there is no such thing as a lone-ranger Christian, just as you don't walk down the street and see a leg hopping along on its own or a fingernail having a chat with an ear: 'In Christ we, though many, form one body, and each member belongs to all the others' (v. 5). When we give ourselves to Jesus, he gives us to each other in a way that properly impacts daily life. We don't just share a pew; we share our money. We don't just pop Christmas cards through letter boxes; we open our homes and make extra room around our dining tables. We don't just offer polite platitudes; we weep with shared pain and laugh with shared joy. It is a messy business.

The body of Christ, the church, is at the heart of God's good purposes for us and the whole world. This is how he intends us to become spiritually mature; it is how he wants his character reflected to those who don't yet know him; it is how he plans to meet the needs of a hurting world. Life in the community of faith is where we'll experience the fullness of God's *shalom*.

For reflection

The only way for our minds and hearts to be transformed is to be brutally honest with God. Bring before him your thoughts and feelings about church. Ask him to heal the wounds inflicted by his people. Tell him what you find hard, what you don't like and why you'd rather not get involved. Ask him to show you how he sees this body, with all its quirks and failings.

Prayer

Lord, thank you that you made all who believe in you a family.
Thank you that we belong to you, and we belong to each other.
Please increase my love, commitment and loyalty to the church.
In the precious name of your Son Jesus, Amen

31 December

Dual citizenship

Once, on being asked by the Pharisees when the kingdom of God would come, Jesus replied, 'The coming of the kingdom of God is not something that can be observed, nor will people say, "Here it is," or "There it is," because the kingdom of God is in your midst.'

Then he said to his disciples, 'The time is coming when you will long to see one of the days of the Son of Man, but you will not see it. People will tell you, "There he is!" or "Here he is!" Do not go running off after them. For the Son of Man in his day will be like the lightning, which flashes and lights up the sky from one end to the other. But first he must suffer many things and be rejected by this generation.'
LUKE 17:20–25

My daughters have dual UK/US citizenship, thanks to their English mother and American father. I'm the only one in the family with a single passport. Should they wish, the girls could go and live in America, where they would have the right to work, access public services and vote. They'd be required to pay taxes, obey the laws and support the Constitution. Or they could choose to stay here, with me. I'm not going to pretend I don't have an opinion on this decision!

Citizenship is laden with rights and responsibilities. It calls us to submit to specific leadership, to live according to a communal set of expectations and to contribute to an enterprise far greater than the fulfilment of personal ambition. As a citizen, we gain protection, belonging and resources.

Jesus talked a lot about 'the kingdom of God'. His three-year public ministry was largely devoted to announcing its arrival, explaining its boundary and cultures, inviting people into it and claiming in word and deed to be its ruler. When we belong to Jesus, we are citizens of his kingdom, so this is an important concept for us to explore.

As we do, we will have to hold some ideas in tension with each other. We'll look at three pairs of these apparently competing ideas in a moment, but first a thought: the Pharisees and the disciples often struggled to understand mysterious spiritual realities, so we shouldn't be surprised or concerned if we do too. When I am tempted to be discouraged at my mind's limitations when it comes to biblical teaching, I remember that I struggle with basic maths which others could do in their sleep. Just because I don't understand it doesn't mean there isn't logic and sense within it, accessible to a greater mind than mine. The greatest of all minds is God's. I am glad God is so far beyond me in every way. It makes me feel safe.

The first pair of ideas is that the kingdom of God came with Jesus and is a present reality, in our midst (v. 21); it is also something we are still waiting for (v. 22). The second: Jesus, aka the Son of Man, is a rejected and suffering servant; he is also the ruler of all, whose return in glory will 'light up the sky from one end to another' (v. 24). And third: the kingdom cannot be observed or geographically located (vv. 20–21); but it can be found by those who search for it: 'Seek and you will find; knock and the door will be opened to you' (Matthew 7:7).

For reflection

Our citizenship of this kingdom carries weighty responsibilities and incredible privileges. Make a list of some that come to mind.

Prayer

One of our responsibilities (in partnership with the Holy Spirit) is to expand the boundaries of the kingdom, gathering in more and more people to a place of eternal safety under a just and loving king. As Jesus taught us, let's pray:

May your kingdom come, on earth as it is in heaven. Amen

1 January

A new way

That, however, is not the way of life you learned when you heard about Christ and were taught in him in accordance with the truth that is in Jesus. You were taught, with regard to your former way of life, to put off your old self, which is being corrupted by its deceitful desires; to be made new in the attitude of your minds; and to put on the new self, created to be like God in true righteousness and holiness…

And do not grieve the Holy Spirit of God, with whom you were sealed for the day of redemption.

EPHESIANS 4:20–24, 30

I'm a sucker for New Year's resolutions. I love the idea of a fresh start. The first day of January is this mythical line in the sand which, once crossed, means lasting change. This is the year I'm going to crack physical fitness, keep my plants alive, write my novel and send thank-you cards. Or maybe next year is the year.

I'm not alone: studies show 60% of us make these lists every year. Something in us yearns for personal growth. We want a 'new self', a better one, and we hope that these resolutions we make might finally work. But they don't, at least for 92% of us they don't. And even if they did, the change wouldn't come close to the kind of whole-person, whole-life transformation Paul is talking about here.

So do we give up on the whole idea of change? After all, the Holy Spirit has guaranteed our redemption (v. 30). 'Redemption' is one of those words that has lost its punch in common usage. We redeem coupons and not much else. But in this context, 'redemption' means being rescued from death and destruction, saved from the consequences of our sin and given the gift of a never-ending life in God's presence. The criminal on the cross next to Jesus was welcomed into paradise with the same open arms one assumes awaited Mother Teresa. It is God's prerogative to redeem – nothing to do with human effort. Why make the effort, then?

We make the effort because biblical redemption, as opposed to coupon redemption, is relational. It was God's love for us that took Jesus to the cross. When we even begin to grasp the depth and intensity of this love, our response is reciprocal love. And when we love someone, our natural inclination is to do whatever we can to make them happy, strengthen our relationship and avoid causing them hurt. If we persist in a way of life we know is not right in God's eyes, we 'grieve the Holy Spirit of God' (v. 30). Elsewhere in his letter to the Ephesian church, Paul gets very specific about the differences between how our 'old self' and 'new self' might be expected to behave. Everything from how we earn and spend our money, what we think and say, our sexual behaviour and our emotional life is addressed in the New Testament. The question we each have to answer is: how much do we love Jesus?

We make the effort because we have been rewired to do so. We have been given a new identity and purpose: we're 'created to be like God in true righteousness and holiness' (v. 24). In *The Voyage of the Dawn Treader*, one of the Narnia Chronicles by C.S. Lewis, the vile Eustace Scrubb becomes a dragon, having skived off ship-restoration duty and discovered a cave of treasure which he tries to pillage. This is a vivid picture of the way 'deceitful desires' (v. 22) corrupt us.

We make the effort because our effort is only part of the picture. As a dragon Eustace comes to realise how not only his physical being but also his character is deformed, and he becomes desperate to change. Once he has reached this point, he is able to overcome the terror and withstand the pain of letting the great lion Aslan rip away his dragon-self and restore his humanity. This story has been one of the ways I've come to understand how my transformation into Christlikeness is both entirely God's work done *in me* and also something that requires my full participation.

As a boy once again, Eustace lives as a boy: he can speak, he's hungry for human food, he walks rather than flies. Aslan has changed his whole being, and this being instinctively behaves in line with his nature. But he still needs to take care not to fall back into the vileness that turned him into a dragon in the first place.

Whatever else we resolve on this first day of a new year, let's resolve to put on our new selves every day, becoming more and more like Christ as he draws us to him in eternal love and mercy.

For reflection

What practices and habits might help me to grow in holiness in the coming year?

Prayer

Lord God, I pray that out of your glorious riches you may strengthen me with power through your Spirit in my inner being, so that Christ may dwell in my heart through faith. And I pray that, being rooted and established in love, I may have power, together with all the Lord's people, to grasp how wide and long and high and deep is the love of Christ. Amen

From EPHESIANS 3:16–18

2 January

Peace beyond understanding

Rejoice in the Lord always. I will say it again: rejoice! Let
your gentleness be evident to all. The Lord is near. Do not be
anxious about anything, but in every situation, by prayer and
petition, with thanksgiving, present your requests to God.
And the peace of God, which transcends all understanding,
will guard your hearts and your minds in Christ Jesus.

Finally, brothers and sisters, whatever is true, whatever
is noble, whatever is right, whatever is pure, whatever is
lovely, whatever is admirable – if anything is excellent or
praiseworthy – think about such things. Whatever you have
learned or received or heard from me, or seen in me – put it
into practice. And the God of peace will be with you.

PHILIPPIANS 4:4–9

Peace had a big moment in the 1960s in America – it had a logo, it had
dope-addled, long-haired disciples and it was achievable if enough
people marched and sang about it. World peace was the dearest wish
of beauty queens, Californian dropouts and strumming minstrels
across all 50 states, even as the US became ever more embroiled in
the Vietnam war.

This is one specific cultural lens on peace. Another comes from east-
ern religions, Buddhism and Hinduism in particular, where peace is
subjective, individual and internal. To find peace, a person searches
for nirvana – a state of passive emptiness largely defined by absence.

The angel announcing the birth of Jesus to the shepherds declared,
'Peace to those on whom his favour rests' (Luke 2:14). The awaited

Messiah was to be a 'Prince of Peace' (Isaiah 9:6). At the last supper, knowing how the following days would unfold, Jesus told his companions not to be afraid or to let their hearts be troubled: 'Peace I leave with you; my peace I give you' (John 14:27). There is peace on offer for those living a redeemed life in Christ, albeit a very different kind of peace to that experienced by Tibetan monks or stoned hippies. Let's consider what kind of peace Jesus gives us.

The peace of Jesus transcends circumstances, because it is rooted in his reassuring presence and promise that our security is unshakeable. The command to rejoice in verse 4 is not a command to hold stoical celebrations in denial of terrible realities, but to hold on to the joy of our relationship with the Lord; whatever else goes on, his love for us remains the bigger picture.

As I'm sure you know from personal experience, we followers of Christ are rarely as peaceful as we could be. We can be wracked with anxiety and as fretful as everyone else. When Covid-19 became an uncontrolled pandemic in early 2020, there were several days when I struggled to breathe, woke each morning at 4.30 with racing thoughts, let myself dwell on catastrophic disaster scenarios and spiralled into panic. The peace is there for us, but as Paul writes here, whether we access it is to some degree down to us.

We need to choose to take our situation to God in prayer rather than sitting alone chewing over our troubles. My anxiety about the virus was doing nothing other than making me feel terrible. In telling God my worst fears, I was handing the problem to someone with power, wisdom and clarity infinitely beyond my own, and it helped.

Alongside asking for things, we need to express our gratitude for what God has already done for us (v. 6). Asking and thanking belong together to guard us from becoming needy, grasping, manipulative takers in our relationship with our heavenly Father. A whole, deepening, intimate relationship with God is the ultimate source of peace, so this makes sense.

We need to discipline and direct our thoughts to the pure, lovely, admirable, excellent and praiseworthy. During those days of freefall, I spent hours on news sites and social media feeding myself with more and more reasons to fear, which, as you might imagine, made me feel worse. I had to stop and refocus: 'God is our refuge and strength, an ever-present help in trouble. Therefore we will not fear, though a terrible sickness may spread around the globe and life as we know it come to a halt' (Psalm 46:1–2 and my own addition!). The connection between thoughts, feelings and behaviour is well documented; cognitive behavioural therapy is one of the most effective ways to combat anxiety and depression and is based on the principle that we have power to challenge and control our thoughts and in doing so change our feelings.

Finally, we need to align our belief and behaviour, putting biblical teaching into practice (v. 9). A lack of integrity causes chronic dis-ease and effectively kills peace on arrival. Walking in faith increases our spiritual fitness and enables peace to flourish.

For reflection

Are you experiencing God's peace today or is your inner state reflective of your circumstances? From today's reading, what could you do to become more immersed in the peace Jesus came to give you?

Prayer

Lord God, thank you that I can know your peace even if my very worst nightmare comes to pass. Thank you that you are near – right now. Thank you that nothing can change my ultimate safety because you have given me a life that will never end. Please, Lord, by the power of the Holy Spirit, fill me with the peace of Christ and guard my heart and mind in you. Amen

3 January

Spread the news

Then the eleven disciples went to Galilee, to the mountain where Jesus had told them to go. When they saw him, they worshipped him; but some doubted. Then Jesus came to them and said, 'All authority in heaven and on earth has been given to me. Therefore go and make disciples of all nations, baptising them in the name of the Father and of the Son and of the Holy Spirit, and teaching them to obey everything I have commanded you. And surely I am with you always, to the very end of the age.'
MATTHEW 28:16–20

The Jewish people had been waiting for centuries for a messiah, but no one else was looking out for one. In the event, the birth of Jesus happened quietly and few even in Israel got wind of it at first. Although an angelic fanfare blasted over a hillside, it was heard only by some shepherds. Although there were visitors and gifts, they arrived late (scholars think Jesus was probably two when he was given his gold, frankincense and myrrh). Although his arrival was on King Herod's radar, Jesus made no immediate national impact. This tiny boy was greeted by his mother and her betrothed, swaddled and laid in a repurposed animal feeding trough. So began the life of God incarnate.

Thirty-three years later, Jesus was well known in Israel. Wherever he went, crowds followed. He was sought out by influential leaders and his teaching caused seismic political and religious shifts. He was executed as a criminal and news of his resurrection was suppressed, the chief priests and elders paying off the soldiers who were guarding the tomb to say that Jesus' followers had robbed the grave of his body.

Whatever fame he'd accumulated largely remained within the borders of his own country and surely would now crumble into the dust of ever-fainter memory. And yet, here we are in the 21st century, a living community of the redeemed. How and why could this have happened, and what role has God given us in the continuation of his church?

These verses from Matthew give us some answers to our questions. In verse 17, we discover that although there were doubters among those who saw the risen Christ, there were also worshippers, who believed he was God. The faith we have today directly links back to those first eyewitnesses who testified to what they had seen with confidence and credibility.

In verse 18, Jesus reveals he has 'all authority': limitless power and influence from the Father have been given to the one who submitted to death and overcame sin. In verse 19 comes a command: 'Therefore go.' With this authority, Jesus commands his disciples to make other disciples - people from anywhere, not just Israel. The word in Greek translated as 'nation' is *ethne* and could mean a non-Jew or any group of people with a shared identity. The point is, you don't have to trace your ancestry back to Abraham to be chosen and blessed by God anymore.

Why are there now Christians in every single part of the world? Because those first believers obeyed the commands of Jesus and were transformed into those who bore his image. Because one of the commands was to take his image and his teaching to the ends of the earth, so that everyone had the opportunity to be welcomed into a relationship with Jesus. Because Jesus himself was with them as they did so and remains with us now (v. 20).

As disciples, the growth and health of the church is on us. Yes, it is God's work, but he has chosen to do it through us. We have been given an awesome responsibility and if we take our faith seriously, we can't avoid it. The redeemed life involves actively seeking to draw others to God's mercy and love.

For reflection

Who taught you how to be a follower of Jesus? What made them influential in your life? How, when and to whom do you share your faith?

Prayer

Lord God, I thank you for the people who taught me about who you are and how I can live for you. Thank you that through the years, your church has flourished around the world. I want to be a part of your good plans for the lost and the broken who need your redemption. Give me courage to bear witness to what I know of your goodness and love. Amen

4 January

The messy middle

How long, Lord? Will you forget me forever?
　　How long will you hide your face from me?
How long must I wrestle with my thoughts
　　and day after day have sorrow in my heart?
How long will my enemy triumph over me?

Look on me and answer, Lord my God.
　　Give light to my eyes, or I will sleep in death,
and my enemy will say, 'I have overcome him,'
　　and my foes will rejoice when I fall.

But I trust in your unfailing love;
　　my heart rejoices in your salvation.
I will sing the Lord's praise,
　　for he has been good to me.

PSALM 13

In the story of salvation, the birth of Christ was a climax but not the conclusion. The narrative continues to spool out on the macro scale of God's whole-creation purposes and the micro minutiae of the daily lives of each of us. Jesus walked the earth for a finite time in a specific place, carrying out his purpose to reveal God's nature and defeat sin and death. And since then, we have been able to find peace and wholeness in our relationship with him. But the option is still there to rebel, defy, deny and repress. In some ways, the world was reset by Christ. In many other ways, it carried on just as before. Now instead of waiting for an unknown Messiah, we are waiting for a known one to return. We are waiting for him to bring a definitive end to the mayhem, madness and pain. We are still in the middle of the story, and the middle is messy.

In this part of the story, we can feel God has forgotten us (v. 1). Our reasoning for this assumption is usually based on the premise that God should have intervened to prevent x, y or z or to enact the judgement or solution we'd do if we were God. A less forgetful God wouldn't allow a gunman into an Afghani maternity ward to slaughter newborns and their mothers. He'd have provided the cure for cancer before it killed hundreds of thousands of people. Our enemies wouldn't defeat us and enjoy seeing us in the dust (vv. 2, 4).

In the messy middle, it can seem as though God has hidden his face (v. 1). Not that we can assume God has an actual face, but the metaphor is a good one. We connect and engage with others with eye contact and facial expression. By turning away or looking elsewhere, we convey rejection, disengagement or disapproval – an efficient way of destroying intimacy.

I know the exhaustion of wrestling with thoughts and carrying around sorrow in my heart like a bag of wet cement (v. 2). The enemy is not always without – our own minds can turn against us and it can be a fight to the death (v. 3). The 'light that gives light to everyone' may have come into the world (John 1:9), but darkness is still a reality for so many of us.

This psalm was composed long before the birth of Christ, and yet it still ends on a note of faith and confidence in God's goodness and love. How much more evidence do we have that we are never forgotten and never abandoned by our Father? There is a time to take our eyes off the mess and refocus, as the psalmist does, on greater truths: God has been good. He came into the world he made to save us, and his Holy Spirit is with each of us, reminding us we belong to him. God's love is unfailing. He never withdrew it from his creation, and he never will. We can trust that the story hasn't got stuck in the middle. One day it will reach a glorious conclusion and a whole new story will begin.

For reflection

Tell God your honest perception of where he has been (or not been) in the struggles you face. If we don't express these accusations directly to him, we deny him the right of reply and deny ourselves the opportunity to be comforted and restored.

Prayer

Lord, I want to trust in your unfailing love, but my heart is often a long way from rejoicing. Today I choose to praise you. I praise you because you deserve to be praised. I praise you because that is my greatest purpose. I praise you because you are good and loving and faithful and always will be. Amen

5 January

Ready when you are

'But about that day or hour no one knows, not even the angels in heaven, nor the Son, but only the Father. As it was in the days of Noah, so it will be at the coming of the Son of Man. For in the days before the flood, people were eating and drinking, marrying and giving in marriage, up to the day Noah entered the ark; and they knew nothing about what would happen until the flood came and took them all away. That is how it will be at the coming of the Son of Man. Two men will be in the field; one will be taken and the other left. Two women will be grinding with a hand mill; one will be taken and the other left.

'Therefore keep watch, because you do not know on what day your Lord will come. But understand this: if the owner of the house had known at what time of night the thief was coming, he would have kept watch and would not have let his house be broken into. So you also must be ready, because the Son of Man will come at an hour when you do not expect him.'

MATTHEW 24:36–44

I really enjoyed the first few seasons of the medical mystery *House*, until I figured out the diagnosis was usually sarcoidosis. In one memorable episode, one of House's assistants Remy is revealed to have a 50/50 chance of having inherited the progressive brain disorder Huntington's disease. If this was you, would you take the test? Would you want to know what you were facing? Some of us are wired to find comfort in certainties; others prefer to live with all the possibilities seemingly open. I'd want to know. Remy didn't.

There are two extremes when it comes to thinking about the second coming, and Jesus taught against both.

The first is an obsessive fascination with details that might give clues to exact timeframes. Is Vladimir Putin the Antichrist? Was that cluster of earthquakes on the west coast of the US significant? Or that total eclipse of the sun? Some of us would really like to know. In early spring 1988, Edgar C. Whisenant, a former NASA engineer turned Bible student, published a booklet in which he informed the church that Christ would return between 11 and 13 September that same year. It sold over 4.5 million copies and his prediction gained huge airtime on Christian TV networks. However far-fetched, the draw of a specific prediction was powerful. In 1989, he published another booklet, which explained, 'My mistake was that my mathematical calculations were off by one year.' Not one to give up easily, he published two more booklets, one in 1993 and one in 1994. The angels and the Son didn't know the day or hour (v. 36) and neither, as it turns out, did Edgar. Jesus spoke about signs that would indicate the end was nigh (though not the clapperboard kind favoured by angry street preachers), but nigh is not now – until it is. In the meantime, there is a life to live.

The second extreme is illustrated by the people living in the days of Noah, who were behaving as though they'd not been warned about the flood. There was nothing to prevent them building their own boats, getting together provisions or turning from their evil ways, but they preferred to live in deliberate ignorance. Are we doing the same? Is some part of us dreading the return of Jesus and more comfortable avoiding the idea? If that's the case, we need to come before God, who is merciful and just and has guaranteed our safety from condemnation through the sacrifice of his Son Jesus.

There is nothing wrong with eating, drinking and getting married, but it is foolish to be unprepared for coming judgement. Jesus was clear it was coming. He'd be returning, and there would be a final reckoning. We don't know when the time will be, so logically it could be any time.

We need to behave as we would if we knew that at 1.30 am on 5 June our house would be the target of a robbery: ready and waiting.

The Christian life involves holding many apparently conflicting truths together in tension: the kingdom of God has come – it has not yet fully come. We are in the world – we are not of the world. Jesus is with us to the end of the age – Jesus has left but will return. This is just another one: be alert and ready for the second coming – be present and engaged with the present moment. Both/and, not either/or.

For reflection

How much do you live in light of the second coming of Jesus? Imagine you received 24 hours' warning – what would you do with the time you had left?

Prayer

Lord Jesus, I believe you will one day return in glory, to judge the living and the dead. Thank you that I need not fear that day because you have made me righteous and claimed me as your own. Help me watch and wait, living in readiness to meet you face to face. What a day that will be! Amen

6 January

Over the horizon

Then I saw 'a new heaven and a new earth,' for the first heaven and the first earth had passed away, and there was no longer any sea. I saw the Holy City, the new Jerusalem, coming down out of heaven from God, prepared as a bride beautifully dressed for her husband. And I heard a loud voice from the throne saying, 'Look! God's dwelling-place is now among the people, and he will dwell with them. They will be his people, and God himself will be with them and be their God. "He will wipe every tear from their eyes. There will be no more death" or mourning or crying or pain, for the old order of things has passed away.'

He who was seated on the throne said, 'I am making everything new!' Then he said, 'Write this down, for these words are trustworthy and true.'

He said to me: 'It is done. I am the Alpha and the Omega, the Beginning and the End. To the thirsty I will give water without cost from the spring of the water of life. Those who are victorious will inherit all this, and I will be their God and they will be my children.'

REVELATION 21:1–7

Our Christmas journey is coming to an end. We've travelled far – from the beginning of time to the conclusion of time as we know it. At the heart of everything lies a baby in an animal shed in the town of Bethlehem in Palestine, 2,000 years ago. The story is beautifully specific and local – *this* birth, in *this* place, at *this* moment in history. His significance stretches back forever and arches forward over everything. He is the hero of a narrative that encompasses the universe.

The great climax of the narrative is the fulfilment of all God's promises in Jesus. The best picture we have of what that will look like is here, in the book of Revelation. Revelation is the apostle John's written description of visions he had while exiled on the island of Patmos. As apocalyptic literature, its style and approach are unfamiliar to most of us now and its meaning might seem inaccessible. But we can all encounter its power through our imaginations and emotions.

Before the birth of Jesus, the presence of God was sought in temples and his voice mediated through priests and prophets. The giant curtain in the Jerusalem temple keeping the people from the holy of holies tore top to bottom the moment Jesus took his last breath (Matthew 27:51). We can 'approach God's throne of grace with confidence' (Hebrews 4:16). The redeemed life is one in which there is increasing integration of the realities of the spiritual and earthly realms, and yet however open our eyes become to God's presence and work in us and in the world, we know there is more to see. John's vision captures the moment the City of God is revealed in all its more-real-than-real splendour, becoming the reality we experience forevermore.

Jesus brought healing and comfort to many. He made lepers whole and the lame walk, gave sight to the blind and restored loved ones to the grieving. He showed us that God is compassionate and full of love. But even then there were untold multitudes who couldn't get near him, who missed him by metres or minutes and whose suffering was untouched. The time hadn't come for a definitive end to trouble on earth. It still hasn't. You will have your own proof this is the case – bereavement, unemployment, infertility, loneliness, sickness, abuse. We groan and all creation groans with us as we wait 'eagerly for our adoption to sonship, the redemption of our bodies' (Romans 8:23).

The purpose of Jesus' miracles, both then and the ones that continue to happen occasionally even today, is to show us the intention: we are heading for a future where *every* tear will be wiped away, not just those of the fortunate few. In the new order of things there will be no 'death or mourning or crying or pain' (v. 4).

Jesus told a woman he met at a well in Samaria that what she needed was living water – water 'welling up to eternal life' (John 4:14). Thirst is the most powerful of human urges. We've been created with a built-in craving for what we need to stay alive. What Jesus identified in the woman was a far greater need – for a never-ending life with God. Our spiritual thirst drives us to seek God, and he has promised to be found. While we live in 'the first earth' (v. 1), we will cross vast deserts – times when we can't see, feel, hear or indeed sense God in any way at all. Our raging thirst goes unquenched. But in the new heavens and new earth we will be satisfied by the 'spring of the water of life' (v. 6).

Advent is a season of waiting and it turns out waiting is an integral part of discipleship. But we can wait in hope, keeping our eyes fixed on the horizon, where, as surely as the sun comes to end each night, our God will come to make his permanent dwelling among us.

For reflection

Are you thirsty for more of God? Ask the Holy Spirit to refresh you and strengthen your hope in heaven, where all your longings will be fulfilled in the presence of the triune God.

Prayer

Let's finish our Advent reflections echoing in our souls these words at the end of Revelation:

He who testifies to these things says, 'Yes, I am coming soon.'
  Amen. Come, Lord Jesus.
  The grace of the Lord Jesus be with God's people. Amen.
REVELATION 22:20–21

Grab a cuppa and sink into a cosy chair as a father-daughter duo leads you into the celebration of Christmas through their art and reflections. Considering not only the story of Mary and Joseph journeying to Bethlehem, where Jesus was born, but also our modern-day expressions of Christmas, they point to God's light and life during what can be a fraught and exhausting season.

Celebrating Christmas
Embracing joy through art and reflections
Reflections by Amy Boucher Pye • Illustrations by Leo Boucher
978 1 80039 051 5 £9.99

brfonline.org.uk

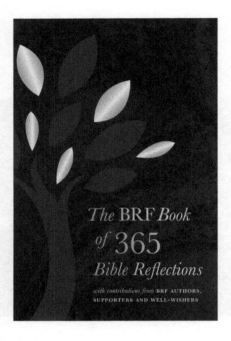

The Bible is at the heart of BRF's work, and this special anniversary collection is a celebration of the Bible for BRF's centenary year. Bringing together a fantastically wide-ranging writing team of authors, supporters and well-wishers from all areas of BRF's work, this resource is designed to help us go deeper into the story of the Bible and reflect on how we can share it in our everyday lives. Including sections which lead us through the Bible narrative as well as thematic and seasonal sections, it is the perfect daily companion to resource your spiritual journey.

The BRF Book of 365 Bible Reflections
with contributions from BRF authors, supporters and well-wishers
Edited by Karen Laister and Olivia Warburton
978 1 80039 100 0 £14.99

brfonline.org.uk

In BRF's centenary Lent book, Sally Welch explores two questions: what is the Easter story really about, and how do we share it? Through each week of Lent, a different aspect of the Easter story is examined: *repenting, changing, hoping, trusting, forgiving, loving* and *sacrificing*. Within each week, the days are focused on what we need to do in order to share the story: *listening, understanding, reflecting, living, telling, sharing* and *becoming*. Each day offers a Bible passage, followed by a reflection and prayer activity. Suggestions for group study and group study questions are also included.

Sharing the Easter Story
From reading to living the gospel
Sally Welch
978 1 80039 098 0 £8.99

brfonline.org.uk

Enabling all ages to grow in faith

Anna Chaplaincy
Living Faith
Messy Church
Parenting for Faith

BRF is a Christian charity that resources individuals and churches. Our vision is to enable people of all ages to grow in faith and understanding of the Bible and to see more people equipped to exercise their gifts in leadership and ministry.

To find out more about our work, visit
brf.org.uk